MARCO POLO

D1633090

MALLORCA

SWITZERLAND

FRANCE

ITALY

Bilbao

ANDORRA

MC

Madrid

Barcelona

Corsica
(F)

SPAIN

Mallorca

Valencia

Sardinia
(I)

The Balearics

The
Mediterranean

ALGERIA

SYMBOLS

INSIDER TIP	Insider Tip
★	Highlight
●●●●	Best of ...
🌤	Scenic view
🙂	Responsible travel: for eco-logical or fair trade aspects
(*)	Telephone numbers that are not toll-free

PRICE CATEGORIES HOTELS

Expensive	over 120 euros
Moderate	70–120 euros
Budget	under 70 euros

Price for a double room,
without breakfast,
in the high season

PRICE CATEGORIES RESTAURANTS

Expensive	over 35 euros
Moderate	20–35 euros
Budget	under 20 euros

Prices are for a meal with
starter, main course and
dessert, excluding drinks

On the cover: Caribbean flair in the Mediterranean: p. 67 | Where the 'in-crowd' meet: p. 43

CONTENTS

The South → p. 64

The Centre → p. 74

Palma and the West → p. 82

Road Atlas → p. 136

DID YOU KNOW?
Timeline → p. 12
Tarjeta verde → p. 22
Local specialities → p. 26
Guided tours → p. 93
Books & films → p. 96
Ramón Llull → p. 102
Currency converter → p. 127

MAPS IN THE GUIDEBOOK
(138 A1) Page numbers and coordinates refer to the road atlas
(0) Site/address located off the map coordinates are also given for places that are not marked on the road atlas
(U A1) Refers to the map inside the back cover

INSIDE BACK COVER: PULL-OUT MAP →

PULL-OUT MAP
(*A–B 2–3*) Refers to the removable pull-out map
(*a–b 2–3*) Refers to additional insert maps on the pull-out map

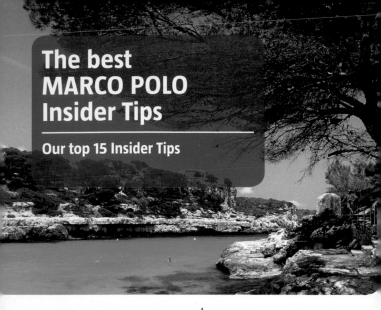

The best
MARCO POLO
Insider Tips

Our top 15 Insider Tips

INSIDER TIP **A feast for eyes and ears**
Sensational fireworks in honour of the Virgen del Carmen in Can Picafort → **p. 121**

INSIDER TIP **Encounter of the third kind**
Travel 3700 years back in time in 20 minutes on a beach walk from Can Picafort to Son Real, City of the Dead → **p. 41**

INSIDER TIP **Ancient shell, chic inside**
A medieval monastery has been turned into the modern luxury hotel Son Brull → **p. 50**

INSIDER TIP **Magic mountain**
Depending on the time of year and the position of the sun, the Cavall Bernat mountain range in Cala Sant Vicenç appears in different colours, chameleon-style. On February and March afternoons, the shadow on the mountain face takes on the shape of a rider on horseback: a popular inspiration for countless painters and photographers → **p. 50**

INSIDER TIP **Salt flowers and organic ice cream**
On the way to the beach of es Trenc, you can buy not only the most recent flavoured salt creations straight from the Salines de Llevant, but also a picnic hamper with healthy treats for a day at the beach, and pick up an organic ice cream on the way back → **p. 73**

INSIDER TIP **Snow white and cobalt blue**
Accompanied by the aroma of rosemary and the chatter of cicadas, a 20-minute walk leads from the remote settlement of Cala s'Amunia to the hidden-away natural beach and deep-blue waters of Sa Comuna: no hotel, not even a beach shack, and usually not a soul about (see photo on left) → **p. 70**

INSIDER TIP **Fresh off the hook**
Be spoilt for choice at the counters of the grill restaurants Can Jordi and Casa Fernando in Ciutat Jardí, groaning under their fishy load → **p. 94**

BEST OF ...

FOR FREE

● *Straight from sea to port*

A fascinating sight for visitors young and old is the arrival of the fishing boats in the picture-postcard port of Cala Figuera: watch crates of freshly caught fish and seafood being hauled from the boats to be sold on the quay → p. 70

● *Surprises in the city wall*

Directly below the cathedral, the old fortification wall houses the Museu de Mallorca. Changing art exhibitions in the beautiful vaults and concerts on the experimental stage in the atmospheric courtyard make this museum well worth a visit → p. 86

● *Cemetery by the sea*

The necropolis of Son Real with its 110 tombs borders right onto the water and is nearly always deserted. A magical place, an invitation to meditate on life and death → p. 40

● *Enchanted Raixa*

Fall under the spell of the patina of the buildings, staircases and gardens of this huge estate. Built at great expense for Cardinal Antonio Despuig in the 18th and 19th centuries, it is in the hands of the government today and may be enjoyed for free *(Sat/Sun 10am–2pm)* → p. 94

● *Protected lagoon life*

In the S'Albufera nature park visitors can experience near-intact wetlands, strictly protected since 1988. Watch herons, cormorants and – with a little luck – flamingoes (see photo) from the raised observation hides → p. 47

● *Petra's great little man*

They say he only measured 160 cm, the great Franciscan Junípero Serra, who tried to convert Indians, founded half of California and whose bust stands in the Capitol. Retrace the diminutive monk's career in the house of his birth and the tile-adorned alley in front → p. 78

○○○○ Dots in guidebook refer to 'Best of ...' tips

ONLY IN MALLORCA
Unique experiences

● *Red earth and white blossom*

Millions of magnificent pink-and-white blossoms on Mallorca's characteristic red soil: experience a unique natural spectacle during the almond blossom season from late January to early March, near Valldemossa for instance → p. 104

● *Bread with things*

This is the literal translation of the Mallorcans' typical sandwich, which is an extension of *pa amb oli*. Integral parts of this delicacy, apart from *remallet* tomato puree, are air-dried ham, *jamon serrano*, or/and island cheese, marinated sea fennel, olives and capers → p. 76

● *That bit closer to God...*

Every village has its *ermita*, *monasteri* or *santuari*, mostly atop the summit of a nearby mountain, some of them converted into lodgings with picnic spots. In the remote village of Orient visitors can try to connect with the spirituality of solitude in the former monastery, today a country hotel with a fine restaurant → p. 45

● *Sweet temptation*

Not even on the neighbouring islands will you find an *ensaimada*, the coiled yeasty bun made with lard and sprinkled with icing sugar, as tasty and tender as on Mallorca. For proof of the pudding, head for the Ca na *Juanita* bakery in Alaró, which has been going for over 100 years → p. 45

● *Luminosity*

Palma's La Seu Cathedral is the island's emblem and greatest treasure. Particularly in the morning, when the stained-glass rosette above the altar projects colourful specks of light onto the high pillars and the pews, this truly is a place to make even die-hard atheists reconsider... (see photo) → p. 86

● *Our homes are our castles...*

Ochre in colour, rustic and rough are the quarry stones that were used to build Mallorca's country houses. Hundreds of *possesiós*, as large fortification-like manor houses in the countryside and fine residences in Palma are called, have survived the centuries; their architectural style lives on in thousands of fincas dotted all over the island → p. 78

ONLY IN

BEST OF ...

● *Once upon a time...*
Learn about the aristocratic way of life on a walk through *Els Calderés* in the centre of the island. There's nothing of the ‚boring museum' about the rooms → p. 78

● *Shark attack*
The Palma Aquarium presents the teeming life of all the worlds' seas – an educational experience, not omitting the threats of climate change → p. 119

● *Going down*
The island's charms are hidden not only under water, also beneath the earth: in thousands of caves, of which five are accessible to the public. The *Coves de Campanet* are small but perfectly formed. The sometimes spaghetti-thin stalactites and stalagmites are so impressive that they need no light show → p. 46

● *White heat*
Gordiola near Algaida is the oldest of the island's three glass-blowing establishments. Do as the Spanish royal family did, watch the workers and admire fragile beauty from then and now in the attached museum (see photo) → p. 75

● *From grape to goblet*
The *Bodega Jaume Mesquida* in Porreres offers guided tours through the vineyard, combined with tasting sessions that range from a simple wine tasting to a relaxed lunch or dinner lasting several hours → p. 78

● *Not just for Christmas*
In high summer this might seem bizarre to you, but the Neapolitan nativity scene in the *Palau March Museu* in Palma is worth a visit at any time of the year, filling an entire room of the palace → p. 87

RAIN

RELAX AND CHILL OUT
Take it easy and spoil yourself

CHILL OUT

● **Relaxing stroll through the city**
Feet hurting from exploring Palma? Combine a visit to the *Banys Arabs* in the old town with a breather on one of the benches in the lovely gardens: take a deep breath in idyllic greenery and think back over what you've seen (see photo) → **p. 84**

● **Your very own chef**
Enjoy an aperitif on the poolside while a professional chef puts together a meal for you and your guests. The chef will come to your holiday finca and prepare a meal of your choice agreed in advance (at reasonable prices); and will leave the kitchen behind as he found it → **p. 25**

● **Relax with Marco Polo**
Breathe in some sea air for an hour on a harbour cruise aboard the *Cruceros Marco Polo*: there's nothing more comfortable than having Palma served to you from the sea → **p. 88**

● **Chauffeured wine tour**
You would like to visit the bodegas but are worried about your alcohol limit? No problem: a driver from *Vip Car Mallorca* can pick you up and drive you around. Your job is to enjoy the landscape, the lovely libations and a drop of wine jargon – in English → **p. 27**

● **Palma from high up**
You don't have to be a resident in the luxurious Son Vida castle hotel to order a coffee and enjoy the first-class service and unique views → **p. 93**

● **Sheer sunset**
When the sun goes down behind the Tramuntana mountain ranges and the lights of Port de Pollença begin to sparkle, high above at the foot of Albercutx Tower is the place to be. Enjoy this breathtaking moment as the crowning glory of a drive to the Formentor Peninsula → **p. 51**

INTRODUCTION

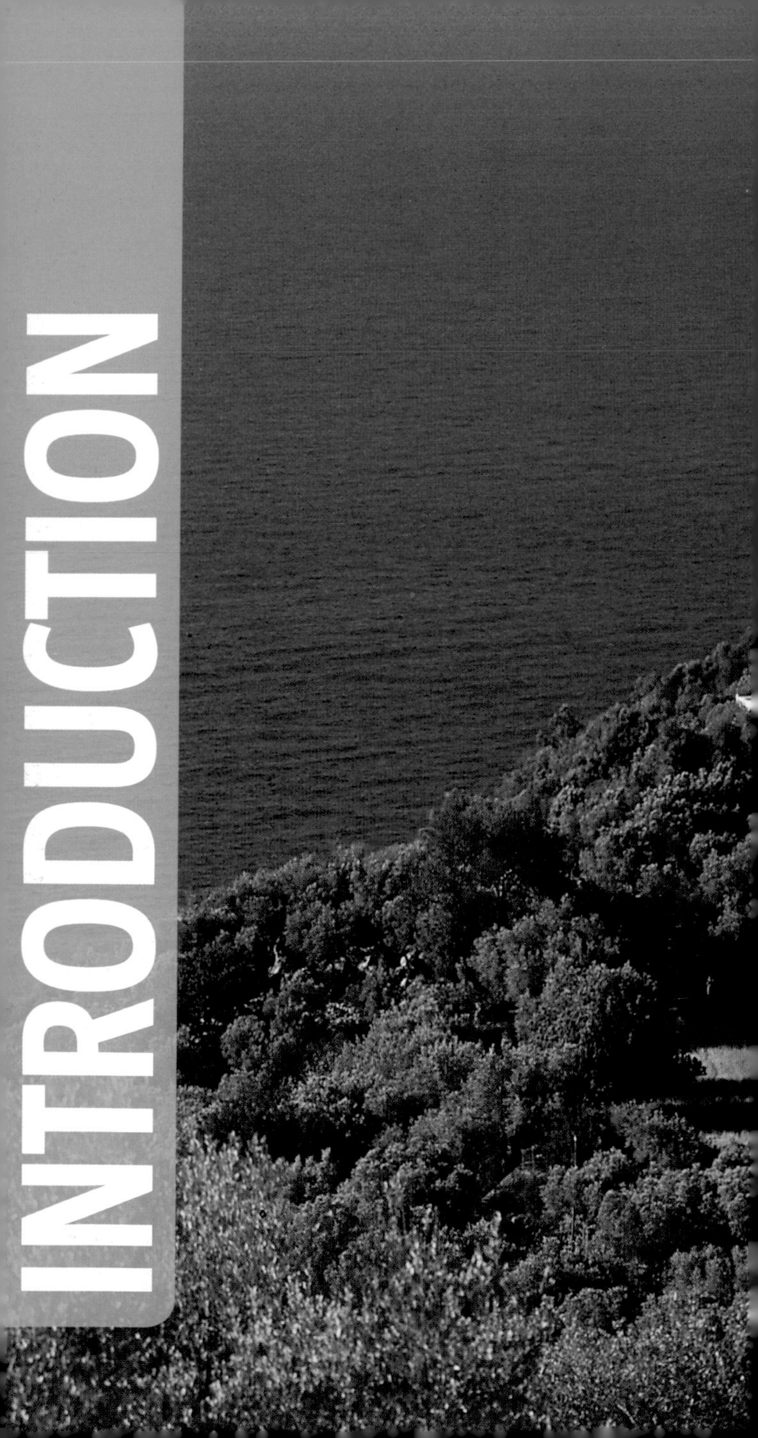

DISCOVER MALLORCA!

Loud chatter of cicadas in your ear and the scent of pine in your nose, the sun burning down on you – and from below, shimmering through the green of the treetops, a turquoise bay with its white rim of sand: the Cala Mondragó is only one of hundreds of small sandy bays dotted all around the island.

And of course this fits in perfectly with the dream image of sun, sand and the Mediterranean. That this area is also hardly built up and has been declared a strictly protected natural park shows ecological insight of a kind rarely encountered in the Mediterranean. Mallorca is a magnet, and the largest island in the Balearics pulls them all in: kings, artists, pop stars, drop-outs and downsizers – and most of all tourists. No other Mediterranean destination is as varied and as versatile. Infamous as a holiday destination for the masses in the early years of tourism, the island has developed into a multicultural microcosm with excellent infrastructure and high-quality gastronomy, without ruining Mallorca's most important resource: its overwhelmingly natural beauty. Visitors wanting to experience this have to be prepared to leave the

Photo: Coast at Deià

hotel, the swimming pool and the resort beach, and to strike out on their own: on foot, by bike or motorbike, by local bus, train or hire car. Mallorca's road network is exemplary, prices for hiring a car no more expensive than elsewhere, and distances from east to west or from north to south don't exceed 90 kilometres.

> **One of the most exciting and most beautiful drives in Europe**

The history of tourism on Mallorca has been both stormy and eventful. For Mallorcans, tourism became the economic miracle with the state-run expansion programme ordered by General Franco in the 1960s, a massive construction boom along the coastlines of Spain – and Mallorca in particular. Farmers and fishermen turned into service personnel, receptionists, waiters, chefs, restaurateurs, hotel directors, bus drivers, travel agent staff and guides. Today, tourism and associated sectors of the economy account for about 80 per cent of gross national product.

30,000 beds in accommodation of all categories are available, from village guest houses through to beach hotels with all-inclusive offers and luxury spa resorts. Add to this the countless private lodgings in apartments, villas and fincas – serving the about 7 million tourists who visit the largest of the Balearic Isles every year.

What visitors can see across 3640 km² is far more than fits into a two-week holiday: in the north, the large double bay of Pollença-Alcúdia clasped between the two fingers of the Formentor and Isla de la Victoria peninsulas, the S'Albufera wetlands and the beautifully restored historic towns of Pollença, Alcúdia and Artà. In the east, the pretty hills of the Serra de Llevant with countless small paths lead down to just as many fjord-like coves, beaches and ports pretty as a picture. The hot and flat south, with its dune beaches and pine groves left in their natural state and its salt lakes is reminiscent of the neighbouring island of Ibiza even further south. Last not least, the cherry on the island's cake: the wild west with the imposing high mountains of the Serra de Tramuntana, counting over 40 peaks over 1000m, fathomless gorges and sky-high steep rock faces, not forgetting one of the most exciting and stunning drives in Europe. Last not least the centre of Mallorca, es Pla, a high plain with a number of still somewhat sleepy villages, the cereal basket and vegetable garden of the

The most famous building on the island: La Seu Cathedral in Palma

island. There is also of course the capital, Palma, one of the most beautiful cities of the Mediterranean, which succeeds in preserving the old whilst creating something new, and which keeps reinventing itself around the clock – with museum pieces from an island history spanning 3000 years and trendy operations such as yoga and spa centres, shops stocking the latest fashions or cocoa boutiques.

Most summer visitors only spend one day in the capital; they have come for the sun, sand and sea and they will stick to it. Over 150 sandy beaches with a total length of some 50 km are available to meet this wish, particularly as the water

The cleanest water in the Mediterranean

around the Balearics is considered the cleanest in the Mediterranean. There is hardly a beach not flying the Blue Flag, and hardly any section of the coast with effluents

1276 Jaume II proclaims the Balearics as the Kingdom of Mallorca; Mediterranean trade flourishes under his successors and Ramón Llull elevates Catalan to a literary language

Up to 1561 Attacks by Turkish pirates

1814 After the end of Spain's Peninsular War against France, Mallorca is given its own liberal constitution

1905 Foundation of the Mallorcan tourist office Fomento de Turismo

trickling into the sea. In any case the island is a Mediterranean pioneer of active protection of the environment, even if that is still not quite enough for the green hardliners. With the massive pressure exerted by the GOB environmental protection organisation on the island government in the 1980s following intense construction activity, the local population also started rethinking the issue. The trend now is away from further urban spread through more and more new hotels and other tourist infrastructure towards a more environmentally sound, soft tourism; away from an overbearing foreign influence from outsiders towards preserving indigenous cultural values. These days, the GOB is no longer fighting alone, as more and more private and also public initiatives are promoting sustainable development for Mallorca. Over the past decades, estates already sold to private buyers and investors, including whole bays, beaches and islands, have been bought back by the island government, and particularly threatened habitats such as the S'Albufera wetlands or the Cala Mondragó were declared protected areas. Last but not least, any construction in the entire Tramuntana, which after all constitutes a third of the island, is subject to very strict limitations. The island council's application to have the mountain range included in the UNESCO World Heritage list is part of this concept. Entire villages, such as Biniaraix, are listed, and 2010 saw the opening of the first carefully regulated organic weekly market in Palma.

A fascinating interplay of mountains and sea

Leaving aside skiing and sledging there is nothing that you can't do on Mallorca. There are over 40 marinas, and water sports enthusiasts will find a wealth of facilities for sailing, windsurfing and diving. Visitors who don't want to be their own captain can book a boat tour, from half an hour with a simple pedal-powered boat through comfortable sightseeing tours aboard a pleasure steamer to an entire week cruising around the island on a yacht. One holiday is not enough to try out all 23 golf links. Both cyclists in colourful shorts and bikers enthuse about all the bendy mountain roads, and hikers just can't get enough of the fascinating interplay of mountains and sea.

Over 6000 restaurants, cafés and bars offer a broad range of culinary treats for all tastes and budgets. Gourmets can feast to their heart's content (and expensively) in

From 1960 onwards: after the construction of the first airport of Palma, mass tourism starts under General Franco

1983 The Balearic group of islands becomes one of the 17 autonomous regions of the new democratic Spain; Catalan culture, suppressed under Franco's regime, experiences a renaissance

2000 Mallorca's visitor numbers stagnate for the first time

2009 After the boom years, Mallorca's tourism feels the impact of the worldwide economic crisis

The water around the Balearic Islands is considered the cleanest in the Mediterranean

half a dozen top restaurants, while in any coastal resort those on a tighter budget will find enough cafeterías serving good-value menus that change daily or a large variety of tapas. Some like to pop the bubbly in cool beach clubs, others stick to the Happy Hour at crowded resorts. What do the Mallorcans have to say about this? Not much. Sometimes they take a drive to watch the tourists. Over the centuries, Mallorca has experienced a lot of occupation and foreign influence, with the Romans, Vandals and Arabs, with the Byzantines, and with Spaniards from the mainland. Acceptance and integration were always more the way of the island dwellers than resistance, even less so hatred. The foreign element was taken on board and slowly turned into something belonging to the island. What some criticise as the phlegmatic Mallorcan mentality others will see as tolerance. And in fact the island dwellers display a characteristic friendly reserve; interference and indiscretion are frowned upon. For the visitor this creates a friendly atmosphere, with at the same time an agreeable kind of distance.

First-time visitors to Mallorca often can't help carrying some prejudice in their baggage; there have been too many reports, often too cliché-ridden, about the island. That VIP visitors to the

Culinary treats for every taste

island and normal owners of holiday homes talk about 'their island' after only two or three trips may well reflect their personal perception. However, they are unlikely to have got to know the real character and variety of Mallorca: the true charm of the island and its people can't be unlocked in a flash; it is asking to be discovered poc a poc, slowly but surely, the Mallorcan way.

WHAT'S HOT

1 A drink with a view

Nostalgia... The ambience has got to be right. Partake of your morning coffee in Palma in front of the Art Nouveau facade or on the terrace of *Café 1916 (Plaça Espanya 4)*. It's not only poets and philosophers who enjoy a *cortado con hielo* (espresso on ice) at the marble tables set between the pillars of *Café Lírico (Avinguda d'Antoni Maura 6)*. The elaborately decorated *Café Atlántico* is the place to be in the small hours, for tasty cocktails or a cool beer *(Carrer de Sant Feliu 12)*.

Hard-hitting

2

The fashionable new sport of padel, a mixture of tennis and squash, is taking the island by storm. Padel is played with rackets on a space measuring 10 x 20 m and enclosed on all four sides by walls. To try it, head for the *Mega Sport Center*. Cool down after the match in the in-house Olympic-sized pool *(Carrer Dels Fertilizants 8, Polígono Son Valentí, see photo)*. Those who'd rather learn this fast-paced new sport with a teacher can sign up for classes at *Palma Pádel (Carrer Castella La Manxa 6, Palma, www.palmapadel.es)*.

3 Mallorcan music

Sing Catalan... Local bands singing in Catalan go right to the heart of the Mallorcans. Amongst the pioneers are *Katau*, who play a loungey mix of jazz and pop *(www.katau.com)*, as well as the rock'n'roll foursome *Anegats (www.anegats.com)*. To listen to live music in the national language, to the *Es Colomer* pub in Santa Margalida *(Carrer Miquel Ordinas, www.escolomer.com)*. For locals, the place to be is the *Gramola* in Palma *(Paseo Maritimo)*.

What's cooking?

Dinner at home, but without all the labour of planning, buying and doing it yourself... No table reservations are needed for your own holiday home, finca or holiday yacht: the island's chefs will come to you. One of them is Marcus Kaspari, who used to work at *Villa Hermosa (www.finca-gourmet.com)*, another is Caroline Fabian *(www.privat cooking-mallorca.com)*, who uses the available kitchen facilities to cook for visitors or permanent residents in their holiday homes, does show cooking of paella dishes and runs cookery courses at Agroturismo Can Torna *(www.cantorna.com)*.

Early party birds catch...

... the worm at after-work clubbing... Mallorcans have their dinner around 9pm, and the nightlife starts well past midnight. Visitors looking to party in Palma need stamina. Still, even Mallorcans are now discovering the joys of after-work clubbing. At *Marchica* with its modern-cool look, the night starts as early as 4pm with some tapas. Those who are up for it can party there till three in the morning *(Torre de Peraires 1)*. The *El Garito Café* has been home to the music and arts scene since the 1970s, with DJs and live bands loving to perform here – from 7pm onwards *(Dàrsena de Can Baberà)*. It's not only fans of electro beats who are starting their parties earlier these days: jazz aficionados too have brought their jam sessions forward. In the intimate *Jazz Voyeur Club* you may – but don't have to – party the night away *(Carrer Apuntadores)*.

IN A NUTSHELL

ARXIDUC

There can be few other prominent visitors to the island who have been and still are revered as much as Ludwig Salvator of Habsburg, Lorraine and Bourbon, Archduke (*Arxiduc*) of Austria. In 1867 he anchored his yacht *Nixe* for the first time off the bizarre Sa Foradada peninsula, below his future retirement residence Son Marroig. The archduke not only fell in love with the island's beauty, but with a few of the island's beauties too. Over the course of 40 years he was to write over 70 books, in particular the mammoth tome *The Balearics*, which he illustrated himself. He purchased one piece of land after another between Deià and Valldemossa in order to protect the ancient olive trees from being felled by the farmers, restored manor houses and had paths cut through the mountains that today serve as hiking paths. The *arxiduc* was the first to protect the island's environment.

BALEARICS

Some 15 million years ago the Balearic Islands were pushed up into folds through pressure exerted by the African continental plate on the European plate. At 3640 km², Mallorca is the largest of the five main Balearic islands, followed by Menorca, Eivissa (Ibiza), Formentera and Cabrera. Add to this some 190 uninhabited islets. Today, nearly 1 million people live on Mallorca, of whom just under 400,000 are in Palma. Politically, the Balearics enjoy

Photo: Talaia de Ses Animes near Banyalbufar

From Arxiduc to Talaya – Mallorca's cultural heritage in an age of tourism and conservation

autonomy status *(Comunitat Autónoma de les Illes Balears)* in a federal-style system. The *Govern Balear* with 59 deputies makes policies for the entire Balearic archipelago; on top of that each island has its own government in the shape of a *Consell Insular* (island council).

CELLERS
This translates into 'cellar'. However, today, *celler* often refers to cellar bars, former wine cellars converted into restaurants. Despite their high ceilings, and

often huge size, these dimly lit establishments have a great cosy atmosphere, and often serve robust Mallorcan peasant food. Inca boasts half a dozen and Sineu at least two renowned establishments, while Petra's only example bears the simple name of 'Celler'.

CONSERVATION
The first critical impulses for the protection of the environment came from the GOB, *Grup de Ornitologia i Defensa de la Naturalesa,* which was founded

In January, the pink-and-white blossoms of the almond trees are the first harbinger of spring

in 1971 as a bird protection league and has since grown to be the largest and most influential private environmental organisation. Soon after its foundation, the GOB forced the government to re-think its policies. Land already sold to investors and construction magnates was bought back and placed under strict conservation orders. In the 1980s, legislation was passed giving a third of the island protected status and forcing future hotel owners to match every new bed with 60 m² of green space. Saving energy is a topical issue. Hotel groups are looking for ways to save energy us-ing new materials and techniques. The Slow Food movement is also gaining ground on Mallorca, as an attempt to re-gain the island's natural produce for the population and gastronomy. Renowned chefs insist on using only produce from the islands, bodegas cultivate organic wines, and farmers reactivate traditional products and methods, which are in turn partly subsidised by the island govern-ment.

FINCA

Finca simply refers to a plot of land; the term is now however more used for the house on a plot of land. A finca is usually a rustic rubble-stone house, ochre in colour and very sturdy, often with centuries of patina and history. Af-ter many fincas were no longer used for agriculture, they fell into disrepair until in the 1980s British and German agen-cies and operators started to offer finca holidays in their home markets. When the old houses had been equipped with modern comforts, they made a charming holiday option off the beaten track and far from the crowded beaches, right in the picturesque back country. Today, not only Mallorcans, but also foreign second-homers are renting out their fincas.

FLORA & FAUNA

Mallorca is always green. And Mallorca is an island with many trees. Seen from a plane as it prepares for touch-down, the view of the sweeping almond plantations on usually red earth, but also of the mountain terraces with their extensive olive and citrus groves, is fascinating. Almond and fig trees lose their leaves for about three months, with the almond blossom lasting from mid-January to March and the ripe oranges lending the island additional colour in winter. Some 1500 types of plant are known on the island, amongst them nearly 100 kinds of orchid. Summer visitors love the bougainvillea's red-and-purple riot of colour growing across the walls of houses and archways, oleanders lining entire streets and motorways, the fire red of hibiscus and palm trees reaching for the sky. The millions of pink-and-white almond blossoms in January are the first harbingers of spring. They are followed in March by yellow and white marguerites that cover meadows and arable fields. April brings wild purple gladioli, May fire-red poppies. After the first rainfall of autumn, yellow sorrel and wild orange marigolds liven up the scenery. Evergreen oak forests cover 150 km^2 of the Serra de Tramuntana, and in the height of summer the extensive Aleppo pine forests resound with deafening cicada concerts.

The island may be rich in plant life, there is no comparable abundance of animals. There are no larger mammals; what you will find are wild rabbits, field hares, martens, rats and mice, as well as feral goats whose teeth wreak a lot of damage. The island's fauna is dominated by numerous types of insect, but especially by birds. Some raptors in danger of extinction have been reintroduced. At the seaside and in the ocean visitors may spot the greedy cormorant, numerous types of shells and snails, plenty of shellfish as well as many kinds of fish.

IMMIGRANTS

Currently, 126,000 foreigners, amongst them over 10,000 British and about 30,000 Germans, are registered as living in the Balearics; add to this a large number of residents living illegally on the islands. Estimates reckon that already about one islander in four was not born there. Mallorca has become a multicultural microcosm, where people of different origins, languages and religions live peacefully side by side. As only a few European newcomers bother to learn Spanish, let alone Catalan, they usually stay amongst themselves. Mallorcans are usually quite relaxed about this development.

MALLORQUÍ

In Mallorca the first official language is *català,* Catalan. *Mallorquí* is a Catalan dialect. Catalan is a separate Romance language which today is spoken by over 7 million people. After the conquest of Mallorca in 1229 by Jaume I, *català* was introduced on the island. At the beginning of the 18th century, in the wake of the Spanish War of Succession, Catalan lost its official status, which it was only to regain in the Second Republic (1931–36). After the end of the Spanish Civil War in 1939, Catalan language and culture were downright persecuted. Franco's regime decreed that *castellano,* i.e. the language that outside Spain is considered to be Spanish, would be spoken in all corners of the country. The Mallorcans had to wait for the democratisation process and the autonomy movements following Franco's death to be given back their own language. From 1991 onwards the names of places and streets have been rendered only in *mallorquí*, which is distinguished from *català* primarily by an additional so-called 'Balearic' definite article (as in 'Ses Salines', for example).

MIRADORS

Miradors are viewpoints, marked as such on maps along rural roads and prominent panoramic spots. Some are flagged up with a camera symbol. The spectacular coastal road in the Serra de Tramuntana between Andratx and Cap Formentor boasts many such viewpoints.

NATURAL BEACHES

True, there aren't that many of these on Mallorca, but thanks to environmental initiatives there are more than many visitors realise. For example, in the north there is the section of dune beach between Son Serra de Marina and Colònia de San Pere, plus half a dozen between Cap de Ferrutx and Cap des Freu. Several beaches line the southern coast, for instance between sa Rapita and Colònia de Sant Jordi as well as between Colònia de Sant Jordi and Cap de ses Salines. The most famous (and most crowded) is Es Trenc, while the most beautiful is the less frequented Platja d'es Caragol.

TALAIOTS

Talaia stands for watchtower or look-out tower. The derivation *talaiot* refers to prehistoric megalithic structures found on Mallorca and other Balearic islands. It is thought that those settlements, in existence from 1300 BC up to the time of the Roman occupation, served religious purposes. In most cases, the watchtower, up to 8 m high and erected from extremely heavy blocks of stone, would have stood at the centre of the settlement. Mallorca can boast over 100 such prehistoric settlements.

TAPAS & CO.

A *tapa* means nothing more than a tiny portion of a fish, meat or vegetable dish that used to be served as a kind of lid covering a glass of wine or beer. Because tapas are fashionable, often you'll see full-sized portions wrongly declared as 'tapas'. An authentic tapa restaurant will present its wares in a counter-top display. More and more places are now offering *pinchos*, small warm or cold treats, spiked onto a slice of bread with a toothpick. At the end, the bill is calculated by counting the toothpicks. This kind of tapa from northern Spain is increasingly popular in Mallorca too.

TARJETA VERDE

Since 2004, this foundation for sustainable development of the Balearic islands has been offering both locals and tourists the *tarjeta verde* (Green Card). Valid for 15 days, it costs 10 euros, giving discounts of between 5 and 50 per cent, in some places free admission, to many museums, bus and train lines, sports facilities, restaurants, hotels and car rentals. The Green Card, including an overview of all discounts, can be purchased at all post offices. For more information: *tel. 9 02 92 99 28 and www.balears-sostenible.com*

In central Mallorca life is usually much quieter than along the coast

TOURISM

Since the 1960s, Mallorca has lived from tourism, more than any other Balearic island. Some 80 per cent of GDP is created by tourism, including the associated economic sectors. British and German holidaymakers alternate in top position among the annual 7 million visitors to the island, even though the number of holidaymakers from the Spanish mainland is increasing year on year, as is the case for the former eastern bloc countries.

Mallorca's main travel season runs between May and October; in the winter months, tourism is concentrated on the capital of Palma and the island's southwest region. For the past few years the Balearic government has tried to intensify tourism in the winter months, with limited success however. Most resorts go into hibernation in the winter and only reawaken in the spring.

VIPS

His Majesty King Juan Carlos I and Queen Sofia, no less, lead the never-ending caravan of famous visitors to the island. Year after year they arrive like migratory birds: the stars and starlets of the entertainment sector, of film and show business, of sports; politicians and journalists, top managers, models and celebrity chefs, artists of all kinds, bohemians, playboys, etc, etc. Their favourite haunts are in the ports of Andratx and Portals Nous, as well as in Camp de Mar.

FOOD & DRINK

In spite of appearances, Mallorca's cuisine is not identical to Spanish cuisine. Certainly, paella and gazpacho, Rioja wines and sangria have long since conquered the islanders' palates, and olive oil is of course a great staple of Balearic cuisine.

While the majority of hotel kitchens, *cafeterías* and restaurants offer more international dishes than traditional regional ones, a separate *cuina mallorquina* does exist; it has however always been exposed to foreign influences, and still is. In the past this was owed to the Roman and Arab presence, today northern Europeans are contributing to changing recipes and eating habits.

One thing is certain: the island's cuisine cannot be reduced to 'simple' or 'hearty' fare, as is often said. The cooks of 18th-century feudal lords in particular created capricious, delicate little dishes; their recipes are now being rediscovered and cooked by enthusiastic restaurateurs. The only problem is however that even the more rustic cuisine of farmers and fishermen is fairly labour-intensive.

Mallorcan cooking means using fresh produce and taking particular care in its preparation. This type of cuisine doesn't like being chivvied along, least of all using ingredients from tins or the deep freezer. This means of course that the 1000-bed hotel with all-inclusive deals where meals are eaten in shifts in huge dining rooms cannot remotely do justice to the island's cuisine.

Another keen competitor is the barbecue.

Photo: Gambas à la plancha

Mallorcan cuisine combines several culinary styles – and even 'simple' dishes need elaborate preparation

Its triumphant progress through the island's restaurants seems unstoppable, as not only foreigners, but more and more locals too love their meat and fish done *à la planxa/plancha.* Grill restaurants are full both summer and winter.

In places where VIPs, the smart set and status-conscious *nouveaux riches* settle, renowned chefs are not far behind. A handful of Michelin-starred restaurants on the island stand for international *haute cuisine,* for example Gerhard Schwaiger's two-starred Tristan at Puerto Portals and the local cook Tomeu Caldentey Soler at Es Moli den Bou in Sant Llorenç des Cardassar. ● Foreign chefs are increasingly striving for an imaginative light cuisine using natural produce. This doesn't come cheap, nor do the fashionable catering services that pamper holidaymakers who are tired of cooking their own meals in their rented finca (such as *www.privatecooking-mallorca.com*). This does not mean however that you have to pay a lot of money to eat well: given the large number of

LOCAL SPECIALITIES

▶ **albergínies farcides** – aubergines filled with mincemeat

▶ **allioli** – garlic mayonnaise served with meat dishes

▶ **arròs brut** – 'dirty rice' named thus for its saffron colouring; rice stew with three types of meat

▶ **arròs de peix i marísc** – soup made from the juices of small Mediterranean fish with rice, fish and seafood

▶ **coca** – Mallorcan version of pizza with a yeasty dough topped with strips of red pepper or chard

▶ **conill amb cebes** – pieces of rabbit meat in an onion-vegetable jus

▶ **ensaimada** – Yeast pastry roll sprinkled with icing sugar; often copied but nowhere as good as on the Balearics

▶ **frit mallorquí** – chopped innards and vegetables – with a lot of garlic and fennel par for the course

▶ **gató amb gelat d'ametla** – the most popular dessert on the island: a fluffy almond cake with almond ice cream

▶ **llom (colóm) amb col** – Mallorcan cabbage roulade with pork or young pigeon in a jus made from wine, bacon, raisins and pine nuts

▶ **pa amb oli** – (pronounced 'pam-bóli') – slices of bread are rubbed with the flesh of the hard-skinned remallet tomato, olive oil and salt on top – and hey presto!

▶ **panades** – pasties with a lamb filling (served at Easter in particular)

▶ **porcella** – roast piglet

▶ **sopas mallorquines** – no soup actually, but a cabbage-and-pork stew on thin slices of bread, sopas, previously dried in the sun (see photo)

▶ **torró** – pastries made from almond paste, chocolate or nuts

▶ **trempó** – typical summer salad made with diced tomatoes, onions and green pepper in olive oil

▶ **tumbet** – vegetable stew made from slices of potato, aubergine and red pepper, topped with tomato sauce

restaurants and other places to eat, normal visitors to the island will also find value for money and tasty food, without stretching the holiday budget unduly.

DRINKS

As a region of Spain, Mallorca is of course wine country, even though beer (*cerveza*) is gaining ground. Over the past few years, Mallorcan wines were able to recoup their good reputation gained over centuries before the grapes were destroyed by the phylloxera bug at the end of the 19th century. ● *Vip Car Mallorca (www.vipcarmallorca.com)* will drive you to the wineries, so you can enjoy the wines and relax – not cheap, but well worth it!

Most Mallorcan red wines are pressed from the Manto Negro grape. Wine aficionados rate wines produced by the *Bodegas Franja Roja* in Binissalem, the *Bodegas Jaume Mesquida* in Porreres, the *Bodegues Miquel Oliver* in Petra, *Vins Miquel Gelabert* in Manacor and *Macía Batle* from Santa Maria. In the southeast of the island in particular, wineries such as the Gelabert Brothers or the three young winemakers of the Bodega Anima Negra are rediscovering local grapes and ecological practices. Mallorcans drink wine in modest quantities at both lunch and dinner, usually complemented at the table by a bottle of water *(aigo/agua)* with *(amb/con)* or without *(sense/sin)* gas, i.e. sparkling or still. A refreshing drink in the summer months is *horchata d'ametla* (almond milk). For their breakfast, the locals will order a *café con leche* (milky coffee), and after a meal a *café* (espresso) or a *cortado* (espresso with milk). The bubbly is known as *cava* and liqueurs as *chupito*. Salut!

Gives you an appetite:
pa amb oli with *sobrasada*

BARS, CAFETERÍAS, RESTAURANTES

2600 *cafeterías* and 2800 restaurants vie for the custom of holidaymakers, who are usually surprised to see that the olives that are nearly always served unasked appear on the bill, as well as the *cubierto* cover charge, at up to 2.5 euros. Add to this IVA (VAT, Value Added Tax) at 7 per cent.

Good restaurants usually require a reservation; at arrival, when you enter the restaurant, the maître d' or waiter will show you to your table. The bill is usually presented folded on a small plate, on which you can later leave the tip.

SHOPPING

The fame of the artificial pearls made on the island has reached beyond Spain's borders. Pottery, leather clothing, linen fabrics and kitchen utensils made from olive-tree wood, as well as edible and drinkable souvenirs, are eminently suitable for keeping alive the memories of your holiday in Mallorca for a long time to come.

FOOD & DRINK

The incomparable *ensaimadas* are yeasty pastry rolls sold with or without filling. In supermarkets you will find *hierbas,* the bright green herbal aniseed liqueur, as well as a black sweet herbal liqueur by the name of *palo.* The only (mild) island brandy is called *Suau. Tàperes* (capers) are primarily cultivated in the south of Mallorca around Campos and Felanitx. The buds of the pink-and-white caper plant are marinated in a vinegar-and-oil brine. They are sold at weekly markets in any quantity you like, as are olives. The small green, bitter ones grow on the island, while the large ones are usually imported from Andalucia. Cold-pressed olive oil from Sóller is well worth buying, there's nothing between it and the best Italian oils. All these treats are on offer in many places on the island at the ● *fires,* autumn fairs, for example at the olive fair in *Caimari*, the honey fair in *Llubí,* the herb fair in *Selva,* and the *dijous bou* in Inca.

POTTERY

Most ceramics are imported from the mainland. Island pottery is predominantly manufactured in Pórtol. The flat *greixoneras* that are only glazed on one side, and the bulbous *ólles* are used as cooking pots in Mallorcan houses to this day. They are however only suitable for a gas stove or inside an oven, not for electric hobs! Also typical for the island are the *siurells,* which are said to date back to the Phoenicians. These white clay pipes with red-and-green stripes used to be wedding offerings; today they are considered lucky charms. The pipes are mainly produced in Sa Cabaneta.

ART & GRAPHIC DESIGN

Mallorca is home to many arts. Nearly 3000 painters are said to live and work here, leaving behind modest or impressive traces depending on their talent. There are run-of-the mill depictions of mountain scenery in oils, but also extraordinary objects, paintings

Made in Mallorca: there's no need to buy kitsch souvenirs to remind you of your holiday on the largest Balearic island

and prints by very talented avantgarde artists, of Mallorcan, Catalan or foreign origin. Take care when offered works by renowned Spanish artists such as Joan Miró: there are fakes in circulation!

ARTIFICIAL PEARLS

Despite sinking sales artificial pearls are still manufactured in two factories on the island – following a patented process developed in 1925. Prices vary considerably, depending on the quality of the pearl dip, the fastening, the size and quantity of the pearl and its shine. The best thing to do is to get advice from a specialist shop!

LEATHER & LINEN

Inca and neighbouring villages, as well as Llucmajor, are at the heart of a leather industry that is once again flourishing. It is worth looking out for shoes in particular, as they are relatively cheap to buy. Traditional decorative fabrics with a distinctive tongue pattern called by the Malay name *ikats* are found all over the island and still woven in Santa Maria and in Pollença. The heavy linen fabrics *(robes de llengo)* are labour-intensive to produce, hence not that cheap. You can buy by the yard, or sets, pillow cases and blankets.

FASHION

Mallorca boasts good fashion designers such as Tolo Crespí or Xisco Caimari. Spanish designers are particularly creative when it comes to elegant party dresses and ball gowns. The best streets to shop around for this kind of thing in the capital, Palma, are Passeig des Born, Jaume III, and Carrer San Miguel. T-shirts with original prints, particularly with geckos and lizards, the Balearics' emblematic animals, can be found in any place frequented by tourists. Make sure to try on any garment however: a Spanish size 42 is the equivalent of a British size 14!

THE PERFECT ROUTE

HARBOURS, ROCKS AND THE SEA

The harbour bay of ① *Port d'Andratx* → p. 98 (photo, left): a port with yachts, fishing boats, a promenade for leisurely strolls, and fish restaurants. A boat trip can take you to unspoilt Sa Dragonera, inhabited only by birds and lizards. The bendy Ma10 brings you to the two terraced villages of ② *Estellencs* → p. 93 and ③ *Banyalbufar* → p. 93, and a hiking trail leads from here to the hidden port of Port des Canonge. Carry on to ④ *Valldemossa* → p. 104; a visit to the Carthusian monastery is kind of a must, really, but ambling through the lower village, a *coca de patata* in your hand is unforgettable too. The sea to your left, olive trees against high rock faces to your right: this is the way to go to ⑤ *Son Marroig* → p. 44 and, later, to the romantic pile of houses that is ⑥ *Deià* → p. 42, before you relax in the patio of the *Fabrica de Gelats* in ⑦ *Sóller* → p. 51 with your well-earned ice cream.

UP NORTH

Past the island's highest mountains and two reservoirs, the Ma10 leads you to ⑧ *Lluc* → p. 46 (see photo on right), a centre of pilgrimage famous for its Black Madonna. Carry on through holm oak forests, down into the wealthy small country town of ⑨ *Pollença* → p. 47 with a stepped path up to the Calvary and a breather on the inviting market square. A detour to the ⑩ *Formentor Peninsula* → p. 51 with views from the *mirador* and a coffee break in the gardens of the Hotel Formentor is a must.

TRACES OF THE PAST

Surrounded by medieval walls, ⑪ *Alcúdia* → p. 32 is a worthwhile destination for a wander through its exemplarily restored historic centre, and the detour to the ⑫ *Ermita de la Victoria* → p. 36 is a rewarding hike up to the Penya Rotga. Along the Ma12 you will find the finca museum, from which you can reach the largest *talaiot* necropolis on the sea, ⑬ *Son Real* → p. 40, on foot or by hire bike. The small attractive country town of ⑭ *Artà* → p. 36 boasts the most impressive talaiot settlement, ses Paisses.

SWEEPING VIEWS AND TRADITIONAL BOATS

With a tile-decorated alley and a museum, the small town of ⑮ *Petra* → p. 78 in the es Plá plain keeps alive the memory of Fra Juniper Serra, the founder of many Californian cities. Taking the Ma3310, then the Ma5110 and Ma5111 through wheat fields and wine country brings you to Felanitx and onwards on the Ma4010. A narrow road of hairpin bends forks

off to the holy mountain of ⑯ *San Salvador* → p. 59 with sweeping view and a tiny Madonna. Relax with a stroll along the harbour of ⑰ *Portocolom* → p. 58 with its traditional fishing boats, and a stop at one of the promenade cafés.

SHOPPING AND BEACHES

Back on the Ma4012, later on the Ma19, you reach ⑱ *Santanyí* → p. 68. A stroll through the pretty pedestrianised area is an open invitation to shop. Now carry on driving on the Ma6100 as far south as it will go. The small port of ⑲ *Colònia de Sant Jordi* → p. 72 boasts one white sandy beach after the other on either side of the village. This is also the starting point for a day tour to the offshore archipelago of Cabrera. Drive on through Campos and Llucmajor to ⑳ *Platja de Palma* → p. 96 and, if you dare, to the section of beach with the number 6. This is the 'Ballermann', one square kilometre of beach named after an infamous bar, Balneario no. 6, which was taken over by unruly Teutonic tourists. Something to feed the clichés alright.

110 miles. Driving time without breaks 3 hours. Detailed map of the route on the back cover, in the road atlas and the pull-out map.

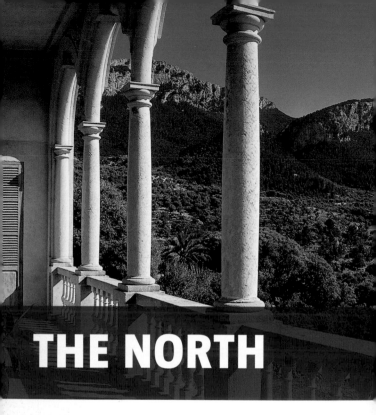

THE NORTH

Thanks to its physical geography and a cooler climate, the north of the island – outside the bay of Alcúdia and Cala Rajada at least – has been spared the excesses of urban spread.

The northern part of the Serra de Tramuntana is sparsely populated. With its holm oak forests and rock faces jutting vertically out of the sea, terraces of ancient olive trees and pretty mountain villages, this area makes an eldorado for hikers and also, thanks to its excellent if bendy mountain roads, for cyclists who like a challenge, as well as for competent bikers and drivers. One of Europe's dream drives winds along some 140 km (90 miles) from Andratx down to Cap Formentor. Its most breathtaking part lies in the northern Serra de Tramuntana. Surprises await behind each bend: the most charming prospects of rock faces, beautifully kept fincas and the deep blue sea.

ALCÚDIA/ PORT D'ALCÚDIA

(141 D3) (ᗘ M 2–3) **Some say the two parts of Alcúdia (pop. 19,000) are like heaven and hell...**

On the one side there is the small country town, its pretty restored houses photogenically framed by a medieval town wall, on the other Port d'Alcúdia, a bit overpowering with 30,000 hotel beds

---

Photo: Son Marroig near Deià

Exciting landscapes in the high mountains, the Mediterranean's largest wetlands – all on historic ground

stretching from the port to the Platja de Muro, then segueing seamlessly to the hotel zone. In summer, this is where it all happens, where British, German and Scandinavian tourists throng the streets, and youngsters fill the pubs and clubs every night. Compared to this, the small town of Alcúdia seems to have a near dream-like quality: cars are banned from the town centre, which allows for carefree strolling, and a large number of restaurant terraces decked out in flowers beckon guests. Prettily decorated little shops are an open invitation for some serious browsing.

SIGHTSEEING

CIUTAT DE POLLENTIA

Pollentia is the main site for Roman finds on the island. In 123 BC the Balearic Islands were conquered by the Roman consul Caecilius Metellius. Around 70 BC Pollentia was founded and became the capital of Mallorca. In 426, Pollentia was destroyed by the Vandals. The new town that rose from its ruins a little further north, under Muslim rule, was Alcúdia. Today, all that is left to see at Pollentia are a few columns and the foundation walls of the Casa de la Portella. *Carretera Port d'Alcúdia | Tue–Fri 10am–4pm, Sat/Sun 10am–2pm | admission 3 euros incl. Teatre Romá and Museu Monogràfic | free guided tour Wed at 10am (3 hours)*

Popular with sailors: the Bay of Alcúdia

MUSEU MONOGRÀFIC DE POLLENTIA
The model of a Roman house is helpful if you want to draw up a picture of what Pollentia used to be like. The museum houses finds from Talaiotic and Roman times, with important archaeological pieces from Pollentia. *Carrer Sant Jaume 30 | Tue–Fri 10am–4pm, Sat/Sun 10.30am–1pm | admission see Ciutat de Pollentia*

TOWN WALL
In 1298, under King Jaume II, work started on the town wall as a defence against pirate raids. Up to 1660, several bulwarks and a second ring of walls were added. The parish church of *Sant Jaume* with its pretty 14th-century rose window forms an integral part of the wall and received its current shape in the 16th and 19th centuries. Inside visitors can find a magnificent high altar with a statue of Saint James, and the small side chapel in Renaissance style, with the wooden *Santcrist* crucifix, which is shown every three years at the procession for the feast of Santa Ana. *In summer Tue–Fri 10–midday, for Mass Tue–Sat 8.30pm, Sun 9.30am, 12.30am, 8.30pm, in winter only for Mass times Wed, Thu and Sat 7.30pm, Sun 9.30am, midday and 7.30pm | admission 1 euro*

TEATRE ROMÀ
Like its larger counterparts, Spain's smallest amphitheatre only managed to preserve its foundation walls. Once, 2000 people fitted in here. The tiers boast prehistoric caves, with trapezium-shaped tombs dating back to the 6th century at the entrance. *Port d'Alcúdia, 200m on foot from Carretera Alcúdia | free of charge*

FOOD & DRINK

CAN PUNYETES
Andalucian watering hole in Port d'Alcúdia, small and always packed, serving a huge choice of the best tapas. *Carrer Barques 1 | tel. 971548352 | closed Tue | Budget*

INSIDER TIP SATYRICÓN
When in Mallorca, do as the Romans do, and experience the joys of ancient Roman culinary culture in the lavishly restored former cinema of Alcúdia (note the fabulous ceiling fresco!). *Plaça Constitució 4 | tel. 971544997 | www.simplesite.com/Piero Rossi | open every day | Moderate*

SHOPPING

The Carrer Major features many small shops and boutiques. The shop at number 19 sells pretty fashion accessories and costume jewellery. *Àgata* at number 48 stocks a wealth of rocks and minerals, and number 34 houses the *Oska* fashion boutique. *Sa Cisterna* at the corner of the eponymous side street offers a well-stocked wine bodega alongside a Mallorcan delicatessen *(closed Thu)*.

LEISURE & SPORTS

The bays of Pollença and Alcúdia provide good sailing and windsurfing zones, suitable for beginners too. The sweeping sandy beach of Alcúdia in particular is ideal for families with children, as it remains shallow far into the sea.

CLUB DE GOLF ALCANADA ☀
This is the island's most beautiful golf course: 16 of the 18 holes boast sea views; the clubhouse has a good restaurant and panoramic terrace. *Green fee 105 euros | tel. 9 71 54 95 60*

WIND & FRIENDS WATERSPORTS
Sailing and windsurfing school on the beach at the Sunwing Hotel Nuevas Palmeras. *5-day sailing course 220 euros, windsurf courses running for 4 to 5 days 190 euros | www.windfriends.com*

WHERE TO STAY

BOTEL ALCUDIAMAR CLUB
This hotel boasts a unique location at the end of the jetty of Port d'Alcúdia, surrounded by the sea. Exotic outdoor pool, buffet restaurant, spa area, direct access to the marina. *107 rooms | tel. 9 71 89 72 15 | www.botelalcudiamar.es | Expensive*

CAN PERE HOTEL
This small but lovely town hotelito only has four rooms, but also serves good-value Mediterranean cuisine in the in-house restaurant. *Carrer den Serra 12 | tel. 9 71 54 52 43 | www.hotelcanpere. com | Moderate–Expensive*

CAS FERRER NOU
A forge has been turned into a small modern design hotel with six pretty

MARCO POLO HIGHLIGHTS

⭐ **La Victoria Peninsula**
A hike to Penya Rotja for dream views → **p. 36**

⭐ **Capdepera**
The island's largest and best-preserved castle → **p. 40**

⭐ **Son Serra de Marina**
Es Arenal: a dip on the protected dune beach → **p. 42**

⭐ **S'Albufera**
Ride a bike through the reeds, home to many birds → **p. 47**

⭐ **Formentor Peninsula**
Sunset at the foot of Talaia d'Albercutx → **p. 51**

⭐ **Sóller Valley**
Charming hikes with oranges as far as the eye can see → **p. 51**

⭐ **Torrent de Pareis**
From Sa Calobra to the wild brook's amazing mouth → **p. 52**

⭐ **Fornalutx/Biniaraix**
Climb up steps in Mallorca's two prettiest mountain villages → **p. 53**

rooms, all styled differently. *Carrer Pou Nou 1 | tel. 9 71 89 75 42 | www.nouhotelet. com | Moderate–Expensive*

SON SIURANA ✿

In 1999, this 250-year-old family estate, which has been in the same hands for generations, was converted into a pretty country hotel with dream views, a pool and seven luxurious holiday apartments. *8 km southwest of town, Carretera Palma–Alcúdia at km 45 | tel. 9 71 54 96 62 | www. sonsiurana.com | Moderate–Expensive*

ENTERTAINMENT

The *Auditorio* opposite the town wall, *tel. 9 71 89 71 85*, hosts theatre performances and concerts from pop to classical (for the current programme, see the English-language island newspapers). The most popular clubs are *Menta* and *Magic* (near the *Burger King* roundabout).

WHERE TO GO

LA VICTORIA PENINSULA ★ ✿
(141 D–E 2–3) *(ⓜ M–N 2–3)*
This peninsula might be less famous than the Formentor Peninsula, it certainly is just as beautiful. The well-signposted road from Alcúdia leads past the pretty villas of *Mal Pas* and *Bonaire*, with marina, to then wind along romantic small bays the 6 km up to the *Ermita de la Victoria*. The locals revere the *Virgen de la Victoria*, a Gothic figure of the Virgin Mary and patron saint of Alcúdia, which according to legend once saved the town from pirates. Dating from 1679, the church appears like a fortress. From here, the INSIDERTIP hike along the high cliffs up to *Penja Rotja* is well worth doing for the superb views across the bay of Pollença, and only takes about 45 minutes. The path is signposted, but does at one point require a head for

heights! Next to the church, the ✿ *Mirador (tel. 9 71 54 71 73 | closed Mon and on winter evenings | Budget)* with terrace and views of Pollença bay serves day trippers. Along the way to the *Ermita de la Victoria* a perfectly laid-out INSIDERTIP picnic site *has an inviting location right next to the sea, a wonderful spot to relax.*

ARTÀ

(147 D2–3) *(ⓜ P5)* **This small rural town (pop. 6800) in the farthest northeast is crowned by a forbidding citadel, within which lies the Sant Salvador pilgrimage church.**
A bit further down, the terraced village is dominated by the equally fortress-like parish church, of Arabic origin. Cypresses and almond trees dot the ochre of the walls with green. In terms of scenery, expect a few fortified manor houses, flowering gardens and small squares, many bars and a few restaurants. Old traditions, such as raffia and basket weaving, as well as the devil-dancing festivals dedicated to Sant Antoni, are still observed here. The weekly market is held on a Tuesday.

SIGHTSEEING

CASA DE CULTURA DE NA BATLESA
In the 'house of culture' the foundation of the painter Miguel Barceló – a genius of the contemporary scene – presents a documented show of his works. *Carrer de Ciutat s/n | Mon–Fri 11am–2pm and 6–8pm*

SES PAÏSSES
This Talaiotic settlement is one of the island's best-kept and best-preserved; from 1300 BC to Roman domination in the first century BC it was inhabited by around 300 people. The main entrance and the exterior wall built from

The parish church dominates the terraced village of Artà

extremely heavy megalith blocks will not fail to impress. The centrally positioned *talaia* (watchtower) is said to have been the abode of the chiefs; a good English-language brochure is available. *Past the abandoned railway station right at Carretera Artà–Capdepera (signposted) | Mon–Sat 10am–1pm and 2–5pm, in winter 9am–2.30pm | admission 1.60 euros*

SANT SALVADOR

Starting from the parish church, 180 steps of the Stations of the Cross, or Calvary (*calvario*), lined by cypresses, lead to the fortress. Under King Jaume I the Arabic *almudaina* (fortified palace) was turned into a bulwark of Christianity. Inside the pilgrimage church the painting on the right-hand side illustrates the handing over of Mallorca to the Christian king by the Arab wali. A number of legends surround the locally revered 17th-century Madonna, telling of how she repeatedly saved the town from pirate attack. Don't forget to take in the view from the surrounding wall of the harmonious semicircle formed by the town. *Daily 10am–6pm*

FOOD & DRINK WHERE TO STAY

HOTEL S'ABEURADOR

This small hotelito run by a friendly family offers breakfast in the patio, a garden and a restaurant serving dinners; another option is self-catering in the shared kitchen. *9 rooms | Carrer Abeurador 21 | tel. 971835230 | www.hotelabeurador.com | Moderate*

FINCARESTAURANT ES SERRAL

Not quite as cosily authentic any more since it became very popular with German tourists, but they come for a reason: fine island cuisine. A reservation is recommended! *At the petrol station on the road to Capdepera follow the sign pointing to 'Depuradora' (water treatment plant) till you reach the end of the road | tel. 971835336 | closed Mon and Nov–March | Moderate*

FINCA SON GENER

Despite growing competition, this rural 18th-century estate converted into a picture-perfect design finca is holding its own. *10 rooms | Carretera Son Servera–Artà at km 3 | tel. 9 71 18 36 12 | www.songener.com | Expensive*

SANT SALVADOR

This stately town house in the upper part of town with swimming pool scores points with its mix of antique and modern interiors – as well as its light Mediterranean dishes served in three in-house restaurants. *8 rooms | Carrer Castellet 7 | tel. 9 71 82 95 55| www.santsalvador.com | Expensive*

SHOPPING

Artá's pedestrian zone doubles up as the main street and goes by the name of *Carrer Antoni Blanes*: at number 7 you will find *Georg's*, with his motto: 'savour all the joys life has to offer'; an interestingly decorated shop selling local delicatessen products, design for the home as well as art; make sure you try the INSIDER TIP *date vinegar!* No. 4 houses the *pedra i flor* shop, a great place to browse for everything you didn't know you needed and just possibly don't. *Can Pantalí* at no. 21 is the island's last surviving basket shop selling crafts from Artá and other places.

WHERE TO GO

CALA TORTA/CALA MITJANA
(147 E1) (*Q4*)

At last – the 10-kilometre access road has been given a new coat of tarmac! The signposted road starts past Artá on the way to Capdepera; though it doesn't quite reach the beaches, leaving you with a 1-km hike at the end. The beaches – connected by an idyllic INSIDER TIP coastal path, which also leads to other small coves – make a rewarding choice for a hike.

ERMITA DE BETLEM (147 D2) (*Q4*)

To those who brave the serpentine bends leading across the rather barren-looking *Puig de sa Font Crutia*, the gardens and the hermitage will appear like a mirage. The last monks to pray and work here moved to their order's headquarters in the capital Palma in 2010, but you may still visit the chapel of the monastery with its avenue of cypresses, and the *mirador* with sweeping views across the bay of Alcúdia. The nearby holy well of *Sa Font* makes an idyllic place for a picnic. *The road begins at Artà Castle (approx. 9,5 km).*

CALA RAJADA

(147 F2) (*Q5*) **This idyllic port, the largest resort in the northeast, and its fishermen have managed to weather the boom in tourism that it has been experiencing since the 1960s.**

This town with its beautiful sea promenade has just under 5700 inhabitants – and about 15000 tourist beds. In summer, a string of fancy boutiques tempt visitors to take a stroll through the town centre. In truth, Cala Rajada, the Bay of Rays, consists of a whole string of rock-lined *calas*. There are many to choose from: broad *Cala Agulla with its fine sands*, the beach of *Son Moll*, small and overrun in the summer, tiny pretty *Cala Gat*, and *Cala de Sa Font* beach, popular with sports lovers. Lined with pines, Cala Agulla is truly beautiful, as is *Cala Mesquida*, 10 km away.

SIGHTSEEING

SA TORRE CEGA

Following a devastating storm, the gardens, a paradise covering 6000 m² above the port, were closed for nine years. In 2010 the sculptures, gardens and the exhibition inside the manor house of 'the blind tower' belonging to the March family were reopened to visitors *(daily guided tours 9.30am, 11.30am, 6 and 8pm). Carrer de Ciutat s/n | Mon–Fri 11am–2pm and 6–8pm*

FOOD & DRINK

LA CASITA
Cosy bistro serving good-value cuisine in its patio. *Carrer des Faralló | tel. 9 71 56 37 31 | open every day | Budget*

ES LLAÜT
The name says it all (llaüts are traditional fishing boats): this eatery on the jetty offers tasty fish dishes. *tel. 9 71 56 35 61 | closed Nov–Feb | Budget–Moderate*

LEISURE & SPORTS

GOLF CAPDEPERA
Demanding 18-hole links with pretty clubhouse, green fee 50–82 euros. *Carretera Cala Rajada–Artà at km 3,5 | tel. 9 71 81 85 00*

ENTERTAINMENT

Spreading out around the largest club in Cala Rajada, the centrally located *Bolero*, you will find a clutch of cheesy tourist Mallorca bars. Trendsetters enjoy the *Chocolate* open-air bar, the *Physical* club and the *Casa Nova* bar, a local institution with its fair share of VIP visitors.

WHERE TO STAY

CA'N PEDRUS
This well-kept hotel with pool and a garden is situated in a residential quarter near the beach of Son Moll. *22 rooms | tel. 9 71 56 51 89 | Moderate*

CLUB HOTEL L'ILLOT
This hotel with 102 apartments 400 m outside the town centre offers the use of its covered landscaped swimming pools with pampering spa treatments to both residents and non-residents. *Carrer Hernán Cortes 41 | tel. 9 71 81 82 84 | Moderate–Expensive*

The onslaught is over: late afternoon at the sandy beach of Cala Mesquida

WHERE TO GO

CAPDEPERA ⭐ ☀ (147 F2) (*∅ Q5*)
This small town (pop. 3500) is crowned by a castle *(daily 9am–8pm, in winter only to 5pm | admission 2 euros)*, the best-preserved and largest on the island. In the 14th century, the walkable sturdy defensive walls framed the Capdepera as it then was, the church, town houses and soldiers' barracks. On a clear day, you can see the neighbouring island of Menorca, only 75 km away. *8 km from Cala Rajada*

PLATJA DE CANYAMEL (147 F3) (*∅ Q6*)
This small holiday resort 10 km south of Cala Rajada has a beach of grainy sand about 300 m wide, with a reed-fringed lagoon. The 18-hole links belonging to the *Canyamel Golf Club* ranks among the more difficult ones *(green fee 88 euros | tel. 9 71 84 13 13)*. Small but perfect, the *Hostal Cuevas (12 rooms | tel. 9 71 84 15 00 | www.hostalcuevas.com | Moderate)* is positioned right above the beach. Boasting a splendid location on ☀ rocky cliffs, the comfortable rural Can Simoneta hotel with minimalist décor has its own access to the sea via a **INSIDER TIP** spiral stair *(11 rooms, 5 suites | tel. 9 71 81 61 10 | www.cansimoneta.com | Expensive)*. The same owners run the rustic tourist restaurant *Porxada de Sa Torre (tel. 9 71 84 13 10 | closed Mon and Dec–Feb | Budget–Moderate)* in a medieval fortified tower on the road to Artà. The speciality here is the wonderful suckling pig.

COVES D'ARTÀ CAVES (147 F3) (*∅ Q6*)
The soot-blackened maw-like entrance to this imposing cave at Cap Vermell is located above the sea. *40-minute guided tours, daily 10am–6pm, in winter only till 5pm | admission 9 euros*

CAN PICAFORT

(146 B1) (*∅ M–N4*) **In summer, this rather faceless resort (pop. 6800) with many bars and shops and a 5-km sandy beach with promenade becomes fairly lively.**
The eastern beach of *Son Bauló* marks the beginning of a protected section of coast.

SIGHTSEEING

SON REAL ●
This rural estate belonging to the Govern Balear island government houses an

Impressive colours of a world below ground: the stalactite caves of Coves d'Artà

interesting museum presenting island life in the 19th and 20th centuries as well as showing a history video on the finca. A 40-minute walk through ancient macchia vegetation brings you to the impressive INSIDERTIP necropolis of Son Real on the sea. Hundreds of people were buried here between the 7th and 2nd centuries BC. The 300 skeletons and funeral offerings found here are kept in Barcelona. *On the Ma12, km 17,7 | April–Oct 10am–7pm | admission 5 euros | www.balears-sostenible.com*

FOOD & DRINK

MANDILEGO
The finest fish dishes are served here in a nautical ambiance. *Carrer Isabel Garau 49 | tel. 9 71 85 00 89 | closed Mon and mid-Dec–mid Feb | Expensive*

ES MOLÍ
Imagine sitting on simple wooden chairs under pine trees, munching the INSIDERTIP best charcoal-grilled *rabbit on the island. Carrer Badía | next to Hotel Sarah | tel. 9 71 85 02 49 | open every day | Budget*

LEISURE & SPORTS

Accompanied hacks for riders can be booked through *Rancho Grande (Carretera Artà at km 13,6 | tel. 9 71 85 41 21 | www.ranchgrandemallorca.com | 29 euros/hour, 100 euros/day with guide).*

ES BAULÓ PETIT HOTEL

Situated some 500 m from the beach in the quiet part of town of Son Bauló, this small hotel with apartments and studios makes a pleasant change from the hostelries catering for the masses. Expect high-class furnishings and good service. *70 rooms | Avinguda Santa Margalida 28 | tel. 9 71 85 00 63 | www.esbaulo.com | Moderate*

PREDIO SON SERRA

Far from the madding crowd, this rustic finca hotel in the backcountry offers a startling contrast to the agglomeration of hotels: an idyllic setting, perfect for nature lovers and horseback riders. *15 bungalows | Carretera Muro | tel. 9 71 53 79 80 | www.finca-son-serra.de | Expensive*

WHERE TO GO

COLÒNIA DE SANT PERE
(146 C2) *(ɯ O4)*

This sleepy-looking village (pop. 500) on the eastern end of Alcúdia Bay some 20 km east of town makes for a good destination for long beach walks from Can Picafort, or the starting point for hikes on the Ferrutx Peninsula. The *Solimar* hotel *(13 rooms | tel. 9 71 58 93 47 | www.hotelsolimar.de | Moderate)* with swimming pool is situated in a part of the village boasting many villas.

SON SERRA DE MARINA ★
(146 B–C2) *(ɯ N5)*

This recent holiday resort (pop. 550) decked out in Wild West decor 8 km southeast of Can Picafort offers (at the eastern end) two *cafeterías* and a small very basic *hostal* (*Budget*). Behind the resort, the little-frequented protected dune beach of *Es Arenal* stretches for some

2.5 km to Colònia de Sant Pere; there are no deckchairs or parasols available however. At the very end of the beach nudism is tolerated. A *talaiot* marks the access road at kilometre 14.2 on the road leading to Artà.

DEIÀ

(138 C5) *(ɯ F4)* **Over half of the 750 registered inhabitants of this picture-perfect hill village are foreigners. The high-minded poets and painters who elevated Deià from the 1920s onwards to the status of an 'artists' village' have long been joined by wealthy finca owners.**

Hotels and restaurants have followed suit. In summer, long lines of coaches and cars try to push through the narrow street leading through the village, and the romantic pebble beach of *Cala de Deià* is overrun with visitors.

SIGHTSEEING

KIRCHBERG ⊱

Flower-bedecked alleyways and flights of steps lead up to church and cemetery which have far-reaching views. One of the artists who found their last resting place here is the British writer Robert Graves (1895–1985), who wrote nearly 140 books. Graves' fictionalised biography I Claudius was written in Deiá, where he lived for over 40 years *(museum in Ca N'Alluny | Tue–Sat 10am–5pm | admission 5 euros)*.

FOOD & DRINK
WHERE TO STAY

S'HOTEL D'ES PUIG ⊱

Quiet hotel on the church hill befitting the romantic village scenery, with swimming pool and fabulous views from the terrace. *8 rooms | tel. 9 71 63 94 09 | Expensive*

ES RACÓ D'ES TEIX

You will eat like an emperor above the roofs of Deià if you splash out on the seven-course set meal for nearly 100

INSIDER TIP ▸ Café sa Fonda: One of the regulars is a grandson of Robert Graves and one of the organisers of the ecological arts festival ☺ *Ideadeià*, Founded in 2010, the festival aims to use the arts, music and film to connect with older cultural traditions.

Once an artists' village, today residence of the rich: the mountain village of Deià

euros prepared by culinary maverick Joseph Sauerschell. *Carrer de sa Vinya Vella 6 | tel. 9 71 63 95 01 | closed Mon/Tue | Expensive*

LA RESIDENCIA ☙

The former manor house, framed by cascades of blossoms, with landscaped pools and dream views of the church hill, offering 53 rooms, six suites and the trendy gourmet restaurant *El Olivo*, is a first-class choice. *Tel. 9 71 63 60 46 | www.hotel-laresidencia.com | Expensive*

ENTERTAINMENT

Tourists, the in-crowd and artists – everybody meets in Deià's only bar, the

WHERE TO GO

LLUC ALCARI (138 C5) (*ℳ F4*)

This much-photographed village of natural stone above the sea only has 13 inhabitants. The largest part of the village is taken up by the hotel *Costa d'Or (40 rooms | tel. 9 71 63 90 | closed Nov–April | Expensive)*, with pool and sea views. In the *Bens d'Avall* restaurant you may feast on the finest Mediterranean cuisine on an ☙ enchanting terrace high above the sea; the way to get there is some 6 km along a bendy road (signposted) to Sóller. *Tel. 9 71 63 23 81 | www.bensdavall.com | closed Sun evening, Mon and Dec–Feb | Expensive*

SON MARROIG ☆ (138 B5) *(Ⅲ E4)*

The former retirement residence of Archduke Ludwig Salvator is today a museum. The idyllic gardens alone make a visit worthwhile. With the permission of the gatekeeper you can use the private road down to the *Sa Foradada* peninsula, where the archduke anchored in 1867 with his yacht and set foot on Mallorcan soil for the first time. *On the Ma10 at km 65,5 | daily 10am–8pm, in winter only to 5pm | admission 4 euros*

INCA

(140 A5) *(Ⅲ J5)* **Mallorca's fourth-largest municipality (pop. 30,000) is much more interesting than its reputation would have it.**

Although the town suffers from urban spread at the edges, it is all the prettier in the centre, with a pedestrianised zone, leafy squares and several good bars, in particular between the Plaça Santa Major, which is fringed by cafés, and the town hall square. The town, since the Catalan conquest a centre of the shoemaking profession, is today still well known for its leather goods factories; their shops however are all located outside the town centre. Excellent bakeries beckon In the town centre's extensive pedestrian zone; another good choice are the *cellers*, cellar pubs serving down-to-earth local cuisine. The weekly market on a Thursday might be the island's largest, but it is also very touristy; in terms of charm, the annual *dijous bou*, the island's largest agricultural fair on the second Thursday in November, has more to offer.

FOOD & DRINK
WHERE TO STAY

ANTONY'S

Restaurant with neo-rustic décor, a tapas counter, charcoal grill and a pretty patio (with fresh fish counter!) next to the leather store of the same name. *Carretera Palma–Inca | at the roundabout past Sineu | tel. 9 71 50 43 77 | open every day | Budget–Moderate*

ES CASTELL

One of seven small fine finca hotels with remote locations around Inca that have joined forces under *www.som7.com.*

View across the natural stone village of Lluc Alcari towards the sea

INSIDER TIP Spectacular far-reaching views from the 'Midjdia' junior suite for 165 euros! *11 rooms | at Binibona | tel. 9 71 87 51 54 | Expensive*

CELLERS

The most famous and most expensive eatery in town, if gastronomically a tad overrated, is the pretty *Can Amer in Carrer Pau 39*. The offerings of *sa Travessa* In the same street and boasting a patio are fairly original, while the mid-range *Can Ripoll* in *Carrer Armengol* offers authentic fare. The fine dishes served at *Celler Canyamel* in the *Avinguda Jaume* thoroughfare are less original, but represent good value.

SHOPPING

Antony's Conexion, Asinca, Camper and *Munper* are the four leather goods factories that sell their wares along the Carretera Palma–Inca. The *Can Guixe* bakery at *Carrer La Estrella* 3 is famous for its puff pastries, and the **INSIDER TIP** *Antigua Casa Delante* at *Carrer Major 27* for its great variety of almond torrós.

WHERE TO GO

ALARÓ/ORIENT (144 B2–3) (*ØⱮ G–H5*)

11 km west of Inca, Alaró (pop. 5200) is a welcoming village of Arabic origins surrounded by gardens and almond tree groves. At the centre, the market square with church, town hall, bars also boasts the ● *Cana Juanita* bakery founded in 1910 and famous for its *ensaimadas.* Centrally located on the market square, the comfortable hotel *Can Xim (8 rooms | tel. 9 71 87 91 17 | www.canxim.com | Moderate)* offers a pool, a garden and its own terrace restaurant called *Traffic.*
There are two starting points for a hike to the ᴥᴸ *Castell d'Alaró* with its simple

restaurant, *(tel. 9 71 51 04 80 | closed Tue | Budget)*: either the mountain restaurant *Es Verger* above Alaró *(about 1 hr)* or the village of Orient, 9.5 km further up in the mountains *(about 2 hrs)*. Halfway up, the mountain restaurant *Es Verger (tel. 9 71 18 21 26 | open every day | Budget)* mentioned above is famous for its lamb shoulder and snails by a cosy fireplace.
The remote picture-postcard village of Orient (pop. 10), which mainly serves second-homers, is framed by apple trees. The former ● monastery *L'Hermitage (24 rooms | tel. 9 71 18 03 03 | www. hermitage-hotel.com | closed Nov–Jan | Expensive)* today functions as a country hotel with a swimming pool, tennis court and fine restaurant.

BINISSALEM (144 C3) (*ØⱮ H–J5*)

The prettily restored small town (pop. 7000) 6 km southwest of Inca was the first region in Mallorca whose wines were entitled to call themselves 'Denominació de origen' for their certified origin. The largest local bodega is the *Franja Roja* belonging to the brothers Ferrer along the road to Palma; you may taste the wines before buying. Right on the church square, *Scott's (11 rooms, 8 suites | tel. 9 71 87 01 00 | www.scottshotel.com | Expensive)* has established itself as a small oasis of comfort with a pool, a lot of luxury and light Mediterranean fare served in the terrace bar.

CAMPANET ᴥᴸ (145 D–E1) (*ØⱮ K4*)

This strung-out quiet village (pop. 2500) 8 km northeast of Inca really comes alive on a Tuesday, market day, when in the *Sa Galerie* bar old and young rub shoulders at the tapas counter. Traditional crafts such as glass blowing, basket weaving and pottery have survived here. Watch glass blowers in action in the *Menestralía* manufacture (exit 35 of the Palma–Alcúdia motorway). Also worth seeing are the bizarre stalactite caves of ● *Coves de Campanet* at exit 36 *(daily 10am–5pm | admission 9.50 euros)* 2 km further north.

white colours of the monastic choir school, have been singing at Mass *(Sept–mid-June Mon–Sat 11.15am, Sun 11am)* since the 16th century. For an authentic and cosy moun-

The church of Lluc convent houses the highly revered statue of the Moreneta

Lluc Monastery (139 F3) *(⑳ J3)*

Against an imposing mountain backdrop all around it, Mallorca's most important pilgrimage site lies 16 km north of Inca in a valley at an altitude of 525 m. Coachloads of visitors make their way to the *Moreneta,* the Black Madonna in the monastery church. Picnic areas line the monastic complex dating from the 17th and 18th centuries. Legend has it that in the 14th-century a shepherd boy found the statue of the Virgin Mary and took it to the priest at Escorca three times. Every time, the Madonna returned to the place where she had been found, indicating her choice for the spot where a hermitage should be built. The *blavets,* choir boys dressed in the blue and

tain restaurant, look no further than *Es Guix (tel. 9 71 51 70 92 | www.es guix.com | closed Tue | Moderate)* with a rock pool fed by spring water and good Mallorcan cuisine, about 2 km outside Lluc in the direction of Sóller.

MURO

(140 C5) *(⑳ E4–5)* Heavily agricultural Muro (pop. 6600) is one of the oldest settlements on the island, having received town status as early as 1300. Muro's monumental parish church — boasting a former defensive tower, today the belltower, and linked to the church by a bridge – is as impressive as the stately old townhouses in the *Comtat* part of town. At their weekly market on a Saturday and Sunday, the people of Muro stay mostly amongst themselves, even though the extensive municipality (pop. 6700) also includes a dozen beach hotels on the Platja de Muro.

SIGHTSEEING

MUSEU ETNOLÓGIC DE MALLORCA

The ethnological museum housed in a 17th-century townhouse shows traditional crafts and living quarters, illustrating rural life in the olden days. *Carrer Major 5 | Sept–July Tue–Sat 10am–3pm, Thu also 5–8pm, Sun 10am–2pm | free of charge*

FOOD & DRINK

SA FONDA

A large bar and a small dining room, a barbecue, and an open fireplace in the winter provide the simple setting for solid homemade fare. *Carrer Sant Jaume 1 | tel. 9 71 53 79 65 | open every day | Budget*

WHERE TO STAY

PARC NATURAL

This three-storey complex with all comforts on the Platja de Muro with its fine sand greets guests with a gigantic entrance: a glass cathedral for sun worshippers. *140 rooms | tel. 9 71 89 20 17 | Expensive*

WHERE TO GO

S'ALBUFERA ★ ●

(140–141 C–D 4–5) (𝄽 L–M 3–4)
Covering 17 km², the natural park situated about 5 km northeast of Muro is the largest wetland in the entire Mediterra-

nean: over 10,000 migratory birds from Africa and northern Europe pass through this habitat of 200 bird and amphibian species, as well as magnificent orchids. Visitors can observe Albufera's natural life on reed-fringed walking and cycling paths. Bring your binoculars! *April–Sept 9am–7pm, Oct–March 9am–5pm | entrance at the English Bridge (Carretera Alcúdia–Can Picafort), information and binocular hire at the Centre Recepció in the park. | tel. 9 71 89 22 50*

SA POBLA *(140 B5) (𝄽 L4)*

While this farming village (pop. 1200) some 5 km outside Muro might not be pretty, it represents Mallorca's agricultural heart and has preserved some characteristics that have long died out elsewhere: traditional celebrations such as Sant Antoni and the rural Sunday market, fringed with tapas bars such as *Toni Cotxer (tel. 9 71 54 00 05 | closed Thu | Budget)* offering spicy regional dishes. On hot August nights, while much of the island dances to the beat of chillout sessions and beach parties, hundreds of music lovers descend on the market square of this most rural of all Mallorcan villages for the INSIDER TIP Jazz Festival sa Pobla to listen to renowned international bands (for listings see Mallorca's English-language newspapers).

POLLENÇA

(140 B2–3) (𝄽 K–L2) **This small rural town (pop. 1700) in the far north of the island has an atmosphere all of its own.** The mostly wealthy Pollençins cultivate their own dialect, traditional crafts, and the arts in general. With a dozen art galleries, as well as the international music festival, Pollença definitely stands out from the rest of the provincial towns.

SIGHTSEEING

CALVARI ※

365 steps along the Stations of the Cross lead to a small pilgrimage church with a great view. *Behind the market square, past the Rooster Fountain (signposted)*

CASA MUSEU DIONÍS BENNÀSSAR

The local painter Dionís Bennàssar (1904–67) belonged to the group around the Art Nouveau painter Hermenegildo Anglada Camarasa. His house is today run as a museum, showing 240 of his works. *Carrer Roca 14 | Oct–April Tue–Sun 11am–1.30pm, in summer also 6–8.30pm*

PORT DE POLLENÇA

Stretching out west from the fishing port and marina of Pollença Bay, the island's most beautiful pedestrian promenade runs under ancient pines and is flanked by pretty villas and hotels from the early 20th century.

PUIG DE MARIA ※

The best way to access this site is to drive up to the city's local mountain, crowned by the former convent of *Mare de Déu del Puig,* and stop when you reach the last houses. From here start walking, first on the road, then on the ancient pilgrimage path. Your reward will be a stunning view and a pit stop at the convent's snug café-bar. *Carretera Palma–Pollença at km 51*

SANTO DOMINGO

In August, the courtyard of the former Dominican monastery (today an old people's home), framed by cloisters, hosts an international music festival; on winter Sundays, Mallorcan folklore takes over. The local museum *(Museu Municipal)* displays finds from Talaiotic times, and a picture gallery is also housed here. *Daily except Mon July–Sept 10am–1pm*

FOOD & DRINK

CELLER LA PARRA

This eatery makes up for its over-the-top decoration with **INSIDER TIP** authentic island cuisine. Make sure you try the excellent paella! *Port de Pollença, Carrer Joan XXIII 84 | tel. 9 71 86 50 41 | open every day | Budget–Moderate*

LA FONDA

Good Mallorcan cuisine (ask for the daily specials) in a restored townhouse. *Carrer Antoni Maura 32 | tel. 9 71 53 47 51 | reservations are required in the evenings, closed Mon and Dec/Jan | Moderate*

PLAÇA

Tapes i Copes is the name on the awning of this new, extremely pretty restaurant with a terrace on the market place – with

the best tapas anywhere in Pollença. *Plaça Major | tel. 971 53 31 06 | open daily | Budget*

STAY RESTAURANT

This restaurant comes up trumps with a unique location INSIDER TIP directly on the jetty of Port de Pollença harbour, light Mediterranean cuisine and a good selection of wines. Lunch set menu around 33 euros. *tel. 9 71 86 40 13 | www. stayrestaurant.com | open every day | Moderate–Expensive*

SHOPPING

GALERIA MAJOR

The most avant-garde of the local galleries shows an extensive network or international artists. *On the market square*

SUNDAY MARKET

One of the most flamboyant stalls of this market sells hats and ponchos with pretty appliqué work directly next to the church. Right in the middle of the market throng you can buy INSIDER TIP organic vegetables at the stall of *Can Sureda,* the finca belonging to German singer- songwriter Peter Maffay, who can often be sees with wife and children in the Bar Espanyol.

LEISURE & SPORTS

GOLF POLLENÇA

9-hole golf links, with lovely far-reaching views from the ☀ clubhouse with swimming pool and restaurant; green fee 40 euros. *Carretera Palma–Pollença at km 49 | tel. 9 71 53 32 16*

SAIL & SURF

Mallorca's largest sailing and windsurfing school also offers boat hire. *Passeig Saralegui 134 | tel. 9 71 86 53 46 | www. sailsurf.de*

Open around the clock: the Plaça Major in Pollença

A break from hiking: relaxation on the bay of Cala Sant Vicenç

WHERE TO STAY

DESBRULL

Pleasant B&B hotel with minimalist decor and six rooms next to the Santo Domingo monastery. *Tel. 9 71 53 50 55 | www.desbrull.com | Moderate*

ILLA D'OR

Traditional establishment with swimming pool and beauty spa at the end of the promenade; a good ☀ terrace restaurant with sea views forms part of the parcel. *120 rooms | tel. 9 71 86 51 00 | www.hoposa.es | Moderate–Expensive*

JUMA

The recently renovated *Juma* town hotel stands right on the market square. *(7 rooms | tel. 9 71 53 50 02 | www.hoteljuma. com | Moderate)*

INSIDER TIP ▶ SON BRULL

This luxurious finca hotel features an unusual, low-key and very modern decor

in a 250-year-old building. The excellent in-house gourmet restaurant *365* (named thus for being open all year round) shares the same design, and has an airy terrace. *At the foot of the Puig de Maria | Carretera Palma–Pollença at km 49,8 | tel. 9 71 53 53 53 | www.sonbrull.com | Expensive*

WHERE TO GO

CALA SANT VICENÇ (140 C1) (*ω L1*)

Small quiet villa resort some 4 km northeast of town, with two narrow sandy bays set against the mountain backdrop of the INSIDER TIP ▶ Cavall Bernat. The *Cala Sant Vicenç (28 rooms | tel. 9 71 53 02 50 | Expensive*) with garden and well-kept restaurant – a text-book example of hotel renovation – is located right in the centre of town. A pine grove with sea views houses the simple family guest house of *Los Pinos (23 rooms | tel. 9 71 53 12 10 | Budget)* with swimming pool. ☀ On the terrace restaurant INSIDER TIP ▶ Cala Barques you can enjoy fabulous sea views with your fresh grilled fish *(closed in winter | Moderate)*. The *Voramar (closed Mon | Moderate)* dishes up the best regional cuisine on its pretty terrace at the entrance to the village.

FORMENTOR PENINSULA ★ ☼
(141 D–E 1–2) *(ᗯ M–N 1–2)*
The long, narrow peninsula of sheer cliffs sees many visitors. It is worth timing your trip for the early hours of the morning and in the late afternoon, when there is a chance of less traffic. This 18-km dream route can easily turn into a nightmare when at its end, before the cape, the multitude of tourist coaches and rental cars can no longer move forwards or backwards. Of more interest than the cape itself is the ☼ *mirador* on the pass with the photogenic rocky islet of *Es Colomer*, the steep 200m-high rock faces and the ● pirate tower *Talaia d'Albercutx* opposite. The ascent takes around half and hour and is rewarded with 360-degree panoramic views across half the island, and the most spectacular sunset for miles around. The famous sandy beach of *Cala Pi* at the no less famous hotel *Barceló Formentor (127 rooms, 16 suites | Platja de Formentor | tel. 9 71 89 91 01 | www.hotelbarceloformentor.com | Expensive)* is pretty but narrow, usually attracting too many people. More secluded (if only reachable on foot) are the two natural bays of *Cala Figuera* and *Cala Murta*.

SÓLLER

(144 A1) *(ᗯ G4)* **Once, this small town (pop. 1400) enclosed by massive summits reaching thousands of metres was an island within the island, until 1912, when the narrow-gauge railway which now seems so quaint established the comfortable connection to Palma.**

The second historic mode of transport is a tram with open wagons, which every half hour starts making its gentle way from Sóller to the port, 5 km away *(ticket 5 euros)*. Both the town and the port suffer from traffic problems, as the alleyways dating back to Arabic times are narrow, and the surrounding terraced citrus fruit groves don't allow for any expansion. Day visitors should let the train take the strain and choose the romantic access route from Palma by the *Ferrocarril de Sóller (return ticket 17 euros | tel. (*)9 71 18 20 27 | www.trendesoller. com)*. For drivers access to the town is through a tunnel with toll or – slower but pleasanter and ● toll-free – over the Coll de Sóller pass. The ★ *Sóller Valley* is particularly charming between October and May when the oranges are ripening.

SIGHTSEEING

JARDÍ BOTÀNIC DE SÓLLER
The Sóllerics' strong connection with their homeland also finds expression in the botanical gardens on the edge of town. Panels explain the plants of the Canary and Mediterranean islands. *At km 30.5 along the country road between Palma and Port de Sóller | www.jardibotanicdesoller.org | Tue–Sat 10am to 6pm, Sun 10am–2pm | admission 5 euros*

OIL MILLS
Sóller is famous for its olives; the town possesses two *tafonas* (oil mills) that admit visitors. The *Oli d'Oliva Verge* is produced by the *Cooperativa Agricola Sant Bartomeu* along the road from Sóller to Fornalutx *(www.cooperativasoller.com)*. *Can Det, Carrer Ozonas 8,* is where the oil of the same name is pressed. English-language guided tours are available by previous appointment, *tel. 9 71 18 20 27*.

S'ATIC

Rooftop restaurant above the Los Geranios hotel with harbour views and gourmet Mediterranean cuisine. What about a INSIDER TIP *seven- course set meal* for 35 euros?! *Paseo de la Playa 15 | tel. 9 71 18 20 27 | closed Mon and Nov–Feb | Expensive*

CA'S XORC

This finca converted into a fine country hotel of excellent taste might be difficult to reach, but provides a true idyll with its beautiful gardens. The quality of the dishes is a bit variable unfortunately. *12 rooms | Carretera de Deià | at km 56.1 | tel. 9 71 18 20 27 | www.casxorc.com | closed mid-Nov–mid Dec | Expensive*

ES CANYIS

Small restaurant on the harbour beach serving fresh fish straight off the boat.

LOW BUDGET

▶ An overnight stay in one of the 100 former monks' cells in the convent of *Lluc, tel. 9 71 87 15 25*, will only set you back 27 euros (for two people), including central heating and a bathroom.

▶ A visit to the really worthwhile *Museu Etnològic* in the Old Town of Muro is free of charge.

▶ Every Tuesday is a free open day at the *Fundación Ben Jakober* at Alcúdia. Both the rose garden and the finca itself are well worth a visit.

Passeig de sa Platja 32 | tel. 9 71 18 20 27 | www.escanyis.es | closed evenings and Mon | Moderate

ES PORT

Renovated pleasant traditional hotel with two pools, a spa and garden in the second row of houses behind the port of Sóller. *156 rooms | Carrer Antoni Montis s/n | tel. 9 71 18 20 27 | www.hotelesport. com | Moderate – Expensive*

SHOPPING

FET A SÓLLER ☺

The products of this delicatessen, such as olive or orange marmalade are made in Sóller. They will also deliver 10 kg of fresh oranges INSIDER TIP to your home, free of charge. *Opposite the market halls*

SA FÀBRICA DE GELATS

The fame of this ice-cream producer ranges far and wide across the island. Choose between 40 flavours, which can be savoured on a pretty patio. *Opposite the market halls*

WHERE TO GO

SA CALOBRA (139 E3) (*Ɱ H3*)

Every one of the three ways of reaching the rock-fringed mouth of the ★ *Torrent de Pareis* is spectacular. Choose between a drive over 14 km of hairpin bends, ascending 800 m, a one-hour boat trip from Port de Sóller past a backdrop of gigantic rocks, or a challenging climbing expedition from Escorca through the 4-km canyon of the Torrent de Pareis. Lasting over six hours, this option should only be attempted in dry months and by experienced hikers. The scree-lined mouth of the wild brook at Sa Calobra, accessible through two pedestrian tunnels (about 200 m long), attracts many visitors. Expect crowds in the restaurants and payable car park (around 5 euros, depending on the length of stay). **INSIDER TIP** Very early in the morning and after 5 o'clock (in the summer) there is a chance to enjoy the landscape in a more relaxed way.

above Sóller. The two flower-bedecked villages with their many famous steps are connected by a pretty a high-level path. The *Can Reus* hotel *(Carrer Alba 26 | tel. 9 71 63 11 74 | Moderate)* is a 200-year-old restored townhouse with swimming pool, a garden and views down into

The tram connecting Sóller with the port, 5 km away

EMBALSE DE CÚBER
(139 D–E4) *(∅ G–H4)*

Together with the neighbouring *Embalse de Gorg Blau* this dammed reservoir below Puig Major supplies the city of Palma with drinking water. From the reservoir's banks it is a two-hour hike up to the mountain refuge *Tossals Verds* (540 m), an ideal base for mountain walks. *30 sleeping spaces, restaurant tel. 9 71 18 20 27 | closed mid-July–mid-Sept | Budget | 12 km from Sóller in the direction of Pollença*

FORNALUTX/BINIARAIX ★
(139 D4) *(∅ D4)*

Fornalutx (pop. 700) is the prettier of the two picturesque mountain villages

a valley full of orange trees. There are eight rooms; **INSIDER TIP** room L'Ofre has a fantastic view!

MIRADOR DE SES BARQUES ☀
(139 D4) *(∅ G4)*

This enchanting viewpoint with restaurant (our tip: try the suckling pig, *Moderate*) situated above Sóller commands magnificent panoramic views of Port de Sóller. From Mirador de ses Barques a pretty but tough hiking path takes you in about four hours to *Cala Tuent* beach. This hike leads past the simple Finca *Balitx d'Avall (10 rooms| tel. 9 71 63 42 40 | Budget)* serving down-to-earth dishes and offering accommodation too.

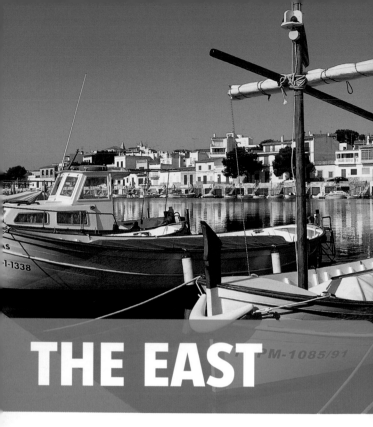

THE EAST

With its white sand, pine-fringed beaches, turquoise sea and white-washed houses, the east coast presents Mallorca's happiest side.

This coast could come close to a Mediterranean idyll, if it wasn't that far too many holidaymakers come here in summer to stay in far too many hotels on the small fjord-like bays, dotted with countless yachts lying at anchor. Apart from Cala Millor/Sa Coma, parts of the Cales de Mallorca and Portocristo Novo, the holiday zones on the strip of coast between Cap d'es Pins and the Punta de Sa Galera have been constructed in comparatively good taste. Even these however occupy a lot of space and have a disproportionate number of holiday beds for the size of the coves. One of the island's most beautiful drives, the Ma4014, runs between the coast and the Serra de Llevant mountain range: here almond plantations, gardens with apricot and orange trees, arable fields and vineyards accompany cyclists and drivers on their tour through a gentle landscape of low mountains. The countless beaches along the eastern coast are only accessible by leaving the Ma4014 here and there to take little paths down to the water. Whilst this takes time, it's well worth it, as all many coves have their own individual character.

Photo: Port of Portocolom

Mallorca's most charming region: a pretty holiday drive connects caves with picture-perfect ports and beaches

FELANITX

(150 141 C–D2) (⌖ M–N9) **At first glance you wouldn't think that the sleepy little rural town of Felanitx has some 10,000 inhabitants – but on a Sunday the market breathes life into the area around Plaça Espanya. The historic centre is well worth a look on any day.**

In Arab times, Felanitx was at the fore-front of *azulejos* (blue tiles) production, paving the way as it were for today's potteries. The former role of Felanitx as a centre of agriculture is still evident, as a few mill towers remain from what used to be a total of 25. Today, the town lives from tourists visiting the nearby coastal resorts, as well as from cultivating wine and fruit, farming cattle and fish, and various small businesses. In 1957 Felanitx saw the birth of Miquel Barceló, arguably

The archangel Michael, patron saint of Sant Miquel church, stands guard above the main entrance

the most important Mallorcan contemporary painter. Barceló's works mostly represent nature; two of them are in fact already on show at the Prado in Madrid.

SIGHTSEEING

SANT MIQUEL PARISH CHURCH

Rising above an imposing flight of steps, the 18th-century church boasts a magnificent rose window and an ornately decorated portal. The church's foundations date back to the 13th century. *Sundays at market times and for Mass*

FOOD & DRINK
WHERE TO STAY

ESTRAGON

Inexpensive, but good: this small terrace restaurant right in the heart of Felanitx town scores with a good-value and tasty daily set menu for 10 euros. *Plaça Perelada 17 | tel. 9 71 58 33 03 | closed Mon/Tue | Budget*

VILLA HERMOSA

Lying on a hill, this country hotel with a picture-perfect garden and pool complex has seen several restorations. Each of the 18 rooms and suites has a view of the sea, even if it is a little distance away. Spa and tennis facilities complement the very fine restaurant. *Carretera Felanitx–Portocolóm at km 6 | tel. 9 71 82 49 60 | www.hotel-villahermosa. com | Expensive*

ES PICOT AGROTURISME

Friendly bed & breakfast hotel in the countryside (at the hamlet of Son Macia 11 km away) with only five rooms. *Camí de sa Mola, km 3.6 | tel. 6 67 73 52 76 | www.espicot.com | Moderate*

SA POSADA D'AUMALLÍA

The Gomila family has lots of experience at looking after guests. The 15 rooms have been lovingly furnished in rustic antique style. *Camino Son Prohens 1027 |*

tel. 9 71 58 26 57 | www.aumallia.com | Moderate–Expensive

INSIDER TIP SON COLOM

The friendly owner of this cosy rustic finca restaurant, has realised that in times of recession fair prices are a surefire recipe for success. His tasty set menu costs a mere 9 euros, on Sundays 15 euros. The generous Saturday evening buffet spread will only set you back 15 euros. *Carretera Felanitx–Campos (Ma5120) km 1 | tel. 9 71 58 05 61 | daily for lunch, in the evenings only Fri/Sat | Budget*

SON MENUT

Country hotel with stud and restaurant. *8 rooms | Camí de Son Negre, access from Carretera Ma5120 at km 7.5 | tel. 9 71 58 29 20 | www.sonmenut.com | Moderate*

SHOPPING

CANDELA

The objects that gave the shop its name are sold here of course: candles of all descriptions. A great mix of deco shop, gallery and café. *Carrer Major 60*

CERÁMICES MALLORCA

Here you can purchase hand-made ceramics such as homeware, vases and lamps with their own designs. *Carrer San Agustín 50*

SUNDAY MARKET

From around 10am the heart of the town gets busy with both open-air and covered markets. There is hardly standing space in the pubs along the palm-lined Plaça Espanya.

WHERE TO GO

CALA MARÇAL (151 E3) (∅ O10)

This is a sandy bay with little in the way of greenery, 10 km southeast of town at Portocolom. A better proposition could be the small romantic ★ *Cala Brafi* behind Cala Marçal, a beach that escaped the construction boom and is only accessible on foot. The way to the bay is a hidden narrow path running along a wall from the upper part of town behind Cala Marçal.

INSIDER TIP CALA SA NAU

(151 E4) (∅ O10)
This unspoilt, deeply indented bay 12 km southeast of town is connected to *Cala Mitjana*, also still largely unspoilt, as well as to the more built-up bays of *Cala Serena* and *Cala Ferrera*.

CAS CONCOS (150 C3) (∅ M10)

The drive through fields and hills to this village with 420 inhabitants is part of the attraction. The village itself would not be remarkable if Cas Concos and

---

the surrounding area didn't offer some fine places to visit. Alongside many self-catering fincas scattered throughout the area, there is also a good finca hotel in the shape of the *Sa Galera* estate. The 13th-century manor house, extensively restored in 1998, today offers 16 rooms and an attached country house. *(Carretera Santanyí–Cas Concos at km 6.3 | tel. 9 71 84 20 79 | www.hotelsagalera.com | Expensive)*. The highly praised, hip *Viena* has lost its founder, who died in 2010; the restaurant however carries on with the same menu. *(Carrer Metge Obrador 13 | tel. 9 71 84 22 90 | from 5pm, Sat/Sun also for lunch, closed Tue | Moderate)*. A few houses further on (number 23), a Chilean family has opened the soberly modern *Rapa Nui (tel. 97 13 96 43 | closed for lunch | Moderate)*. Diners come from all over to sample the imaginative Mediterranean cuisine with a touch of Asia, delicious duck confit and good fish dishes.

CASTELL DE SANTUERI �▸
(151 D3) (*ロ N10*)
The ruins of this massive medieval fortification lie on a mountain 7 km south of town. It is worth braving the bumpy road for sweeping views and the place's bizarre feeling of being away from everything, even if the ruins are locked. The view ranges far across the countryside and the sea, with nobody around to spoil the calm. Some 2 km from the southern end of town on the Carretera to Santanyí a brown sign saying *Camí des castell* points to the badly maintained access road.

PORTOCOLOM ★ (151 E3) (*ロ O10*)
The former port of Felanitx, 10 km southeast with its well-preserved fisher-

The view from Castell de Santueri: a vantage point 400 m high

men's houses and boathouses, as well as many traditional *llaüts* (Mallorcan fishing boats), has managed to stay as pretty as a picture, owing to the lack of broad sandy beaches. Only *Cala Marçal* has gained modest tourist infrastructure. The largest hotel in town with 347 rooms is the friendly *Club Cala Marsal (tel. 9 71 82 52 25 | www.hotelclubcalamarsal. com | Budget–Moderate)*. Otherwise, a few small *hostals* offer accommodation. They have been joined along the pretty harbour promenade by *Hostal HPC* with 14 rooms. Once a week, its light-filled restaurant with terrace and harbour views hosts a DJ for entertainment *(Carrer Cristófol Colom 5 | tel. 9 71 82 53 23 | www.hostalportocolom.com | Moderate)*. Next door, *Colón* serves excellent Mediterranean cuisine with a local touch, prepared by well-known Austrian chef Dieter Sögner, in a refined atmosphere *(tel. 9 71 82 47 83 | www.restaurante-colon.com | closed Wed | Expensive)*. The number of inhabitants (3500) triples in high season, when the residents of Felanitx move into their summer houses. Historical research may say otherwise, but a persistent rumour circulates here whereby Christopher Columbus was born in Portocolom and discovered America from here, lending the place its name.

PUIG DE SANT SALVADOR ★ ☀
(151 D3) *(ω N9)*

The holy mountain of Felanitx (509 m) is a double summit. The higher peak of the two is crowned by an abandoned monastery with origins in the 13th century. The complex shelters a statue of the Virgin Mary from the same period and a Gothic alabaster altarpiece. An oversized stone cross on the second peak and a huge statue of Christ demonstrate the power of the Church. This unusual place was chosen for the *Petit Hotel Sant Sal-vador* with 20 rooms, two apartments and a restaurant; a pleasant touch of the modern within historic walls *(tel. 9 71 51 52 60 | www.santsalvadorhotell. com | Budget)*. A fairly simple meal can be had in the snug monastery refectory, complete with spectacular views all the way across to the Cabrera archipelago. *6 km to the southeast*

MANACOR

(146 B–C5) *(ω N7)* **The island's third-largest municipality (pop. 40,000) gets a fairly bad press in most travel guides.** However, the church square with its cafés and bars has kept an authentic feel; more than elsewhere the centre belongs to its inhabitants, who you can meet on Sundays in the surrounding restaurants that serve day trippers: in the *Molí d'en Sopa*, for instance, on the road to Portocristo *(km 4, tel. 9 71 55 01 93 | Budget)*.

LOW BUDGET

▶ The basic *Café d'es Mercat* opposite the covered market is popular not only at market time on Sunday. The reason? Have a look at the cafe's excellent and good-value daily set menus. *Carrer Major | tel. 9 71 58 00 08 | Sat closed.*

▶ Perhaps you need a new pair of glasses? In the centre of *Manacor* many opticians are vying for business by offering extremely good-value *gafas*. Have a stroll and a browse, while glasses and frames are mounted in one to two hours. *Near Plaça Ramon Llull*

MANACOR

Manacor makes a fair living from the souvenir and furniture industry that has settled around the town, and from tourism. Tennis crack Rafael Nadal, a publicity-friendly figurehead who supports both his hometown and the entire island, comes from Manacor.

In the factories, the pearls are strung by hand

at Manacor. The sturdy building alone is worth the visit. *Along the road to Cales de Mallorca | Mon–Sat 10am–2pm | admission free*

FOOD & DRINK WHERE TO STAY

LA RESERVA ROTANA
Luxury finca hotel 4 km north of Manacor with its own 9-hole golf links and a high-end restaurant. *21 rooms, 1 holiday cottage | Camí de S'Avall at km 3 | tel. 9 71 84 56 85 | www.reservarotana.com | Expensive*

SON AMOIXA VELL
Country hotel in a 20-hectare estate with pool and tennis courts, ten rooms, four suites and one apartment. If you find it hard to get out of bed, you've come to the right place: the **INSIDER TIP** breakfast buffet for sleepyheads stays open until the afternoon. *Carretera Cales de Mallorca–Manacor | at km 3.4 | tel. 9 71 84 62 92 | www.sonamoixa.com | Expensive*

INSIDER TIP SON JOSEP DE BAIX
Six apartments for self-catering nature lovers in a simple but classy farm with pool and its own tiny cove at the end of the world. *Carretera Portocristo–Portocolom | at km 8.4 | tel. 9 71 65 04 72 | www.sonjosepdebaix.com | Moderate–Expensive*

SIGHTSEEING

PERLAS MAJÓRICA
One of the two pearl factories in Manacor, this place produces about 2 million artificial pearls a day. *Avinguda Majórica 48 | off the Ma15 | best time to visit: 9am or after 5pm, as at peak times coach groups get precedence.*

TORRE DELS ENAGISTES
This fortified tower with palace dates back to the 13th century. Today, it houses an archaeological museum, with mosaics and finds from the early Christian basilicas of Son Peretó and Sa Carrotxa

SHOPPING

A huge selection of ceramics is on offer at *Cerámicas y Decoraciónes* and *Cerámica Mallorquina;* you should know however that most objects are shipped over from workshops on the mainland. The decoration at *Oliv-art* (dinosaurs from a leisure park) makes this manufacturer of olive-wood products impossible to miss. Nowhere on the island will you find a larger selection. Through a window, you may watch the carvers and wood turners at work. *On the road from Palma, Oliv-art at km 47 on the right-hand side, the ceramics shops at km 48 on the left-hand side of the road*

WHERE TO GO

CALES DE MALLORCA (151 E2) (*ꔮ O9*)

18 km southeast of Manacor, this hotel complex of over 7500 beds forms a town of its own really. Continually extended since the 1960s, the place lies above several small and beautiful sandy bays, which in high season can become packed. Also, if you are staying in one of the hotels at the back, it's a fair way to the beaches. A pretty shore promenade and green areas make up for the lack of a centre.

PORTOCRISTO (147 D6) (*ꔮ P8*)

This town (pop. 7300) 13 km east of Manacor is a pretty place, thanks to its rounded harbour bay and the *torrent*, with *llaüts* and yachts bobbing on it. Portocristo owes its fame to the largest stalactite caves on the island, the ★ *Coves del Drac* and the *Coves del Hams*. The latter are right at the entrance to the town along the road from Manacor. They attempt to emulate the larger neighbouring 'Caves of the Dragon' by means of a guided tour, a show on the small underground lake and a virtual Jules Verne show *(in summer 10am–5.30pm, in winter 10.30am–4.30pm | admission with digital show 16 euros)*. The Coves del Drac offer no guided tour – leaving everything to the imagination. Here, however, the largest underground lake in the world is the stage for a kitschy but beautiful tourist spectacle: a boat with mini orchestra glides over the lake, which is

Calm waters in an underground world: the Coves del Drac

completely dark at first, then gradually illuminated. Afterwards visitors can go for a short ride on the boat. As the caves attract crowds, it's a good idea to come early in the morning. Access is through the village of Portocristo, then follow the brown sign to the southern end of town *(Carretera Portocolóm | in summer 10am–5pm every hour on the hour except at 1pm, in winter 10.45am, midday, 2pm and 3.30pm | admission 11.50 euros | www.cuevasdrach.com)*. The *THB Felip* hotel *(96 rooms | tel. 9 71 82 07 50 | www.thbhotels.com | Moderate)* is situated right on the harbour promenade. The only quiet rooms are at the back. The *La Gamba d'Oro* restaurant *(S'Illot, Carrer Camí de la Mar 25 | tel. 9 71 81 04 97 | closed Mon | Expensive)* is a fine little eatery serving Mediterranean cuisine; for dinner, you'll need a reservation!

PORTOCRISTO NOVO (147 D6) *(ɰ O8)*
A cluster of several extensive hotel complexes on the interconnected Cales Mandía, Anguila, Romàntica and Estany. The most famous amongst them – and in the firm grip of British and German tour operators – is the *Insotel Club Cala Mandía (tel. 9 71 55 82 55 | www.insotel. com | Moderate–Expensive)* with 545 apartments and a varied sports and animation programme for families who like plenty of company. *15 km southeast*

SANT LLORENÇ/ SON SERVERA

(146 147 C–D4) *(ɰ O–P 6–7)* The two communities (pop. 3500 and 5000 respectively), situated between Artà and Manacor in the Serra de Llevant, share the coast between Cap d'es Pinar and Punta de Sa Roca.

The villages are connected by a very scenic road (Ma4030); most inhabitants are involved in the tourism business along the coast. In summer the unfinished neo-Gothic church of Son Servera houses folklore events.

FOOD & DRINK WHERE TO STAY

PETIT HOTEL CASES DE PULA
Country hotel with ten rooms and suites, as well as a spa, right on the 18-hole Pula Golf course (green fee 100 euros). *6 km outside Son Servera on the country road to Capdepera | tel. 9 71 56 74 92 | www.pulagolf.com | Expensive*. Right next to it, the long-established traditional restaurant *S'Era de Pula* serves Mediterranean cuisine, *tel. 9 71 56 79 40 | closed for lunch Jan/ Feb, Mon and Aug, reservation required | Expensive*

WHERE TO GO

CALA BONA/CALA MILLOR (147 E4–5) *(ɰ PO–7)*
Merged together now, the two resorts (pop 6600) 4 km southeast of Son Servera are connected by a beach about 3 km long, boasting fine sand and a pretty promenade for pedestrians only. However it is completely built up. The mainly three- or four-star high-rise hotels with 18,000 beds are in the hands of German tour operators. The valiant and extremely good-value exception is the **INSIDER TIP** *Cala Millor* guesthouse with ten rooms, clean and bright, in *Carrer Juan Servera Camps 23 (tel. 9 71 58 63 98 | www.calamillor123.com | Budget)*. A thoroughly organised bathing operation plus sports and leisure facilities make the double bay child- and family-friendly. For the past ten years, kids have been learning how to kick the ball properly at the *Super Soccer training*

camp, a football academy established by the German ex-national player Rudi Völler (169 euros for the week). Numerous bars and discos such as *Palace Q*, *Karussell* and *Bananas* ensure that the place stays attractive for young people too. The many cafeterias, such as *Bei Petra (Budget)* right on the beach promenade, have adapted to German guests.

Sant Llorenç into the *Protur Hotel Sa Coma Playa (Carrer Liles s/n)*, Michelin-starred chef Tomeu Caldenty continues to spoil his guests in *Es Molí d'en Bou (tel. 9 71 56 96 63 | www.esmolidenbou. es | Expensive)* with excellent Mediterranean dishes. Our tip: INSIDER TIP the five-course seasonal menu incl. two glasses of wine for 49 euros.

Popular beach near Son Servera: Cala Bona

A laudable alternative is INSIDER TIP *Can Pistoleta,* which puts on a huge and very satisfying buffet *(Carretera Cala Millor–Son Servera | open every day | Moderate).*

SA COMA/S'ILLOT (147 E5) (*P7*)

Separated from Cala Millor by the natural rocky outcrop of Punta de n'Amer is the spectacularly white sandy beach of Sa Coma, about 1 km long, with a pedestrianised promenade. The back country is built up to the hilt with huge hotel complexes. Since his move from

SA COSTA DES PINS
(147 E–F4) (*Q6*)

The well-heeled pine-fringed villa quarter 5 km northeast of Son Servera possesses accommodation to match in the shape of the *Eurotel Golf Punta Rotja (200 rooms | tel. 9 71 81 65 00 | www. eurotelmallorca.com | Expensive)* with its gourmet restaurant and facilities for wellness and thalassotherapy treatments. The sandy beach a bit further south, *Platja d'es Ribell*, has hardly any buildings.

THE SOUTH

A flat, dry expanse, this is what the south of Mallorca is like – oh, and hot of course... The country towns of Llucmajor and Campos divide up the plain amongst themselves, whilst the municipality of Santanyí in the southeast forms part of the gentle foothills of the Serra de Llevant.

Blessed with magnificent white sand dunes and a shallow turquoise sea, the beautiful beaches of S'Estanyol, Sa Ràpita and Colònia de Sant Jordi are almost like the Caribbean.

CAMPOS

(150 A–B3) (*K–L 9–10*) With its tradition of intensive cattle and dairy farming, this town is one of the agricultural centres of the island.

Normally, its straight-as-a-die streets give Campos a rather sleepy air, but on market days, Thursdays and Saturdays, things become livelier.

Campos is said to have existed in Roman times already. The street leading to the municipal salt stocks and the beaches along the south coast are flanked by fields where *alfalfa* (lucerne) and *tàperes* (capers) are cultivated.

SANTA JULIA CHURCH

The star attraction in the parish church is the painting *Santo Cristo de la Paciencia* by Bartolomé Murillo (1618–82); the

White salt works, green pines, turquoise sea: the beaches and coves where the island is hottest have a Caribbean feel

key to the church is kept at the *rectoría* opposite.

closed Mon and early Jan–Feb | on Sun don't forget to book a table! | *Expensive*

FOOD & DRINK

CAN PEP

Despite the crammed and noisy dining room and long waits, Mallorcans consider this **INSIDER TIP** the place to go for grilled fish. The grilled fish platter for 35 euros per head might not be cheap, but it is fabulously good. *9 km south of the town in Sa Rápita, Avenida Miramar 30 | tel. 9 71 64 01 02 |*

INSIDER TIP MOLI 34

Fans of mills will be captivated by this pretty, perfectly restored restaurant in a mill dating back to 1873 with a garden terrace. And the food served here is no less exquisite. Try one of the set meals costing between 29 and 50 euros. *Not that easy to find at Carrer Nord 34 | tel. 9 71 16 04 | www.moli34.es | Mon–Fri 7–11pm, Sat midday–11pm | Moderate*

SHOPPING

FORMATGES BURGUERA
One of the best and most modern cheese-making operations on the island; particularly famous is their *requesón,* a ricotta-style type of fresh cheese. *Carretera Campos–Colónia de Sant Jordi | at km 7*

POMAR
This bakery has been a point of reference on the island since 1902; the most

(Ma6030), km 2.3 | tel. 971650244 | www.finca-amapola.com | Moderate–Expensive

FINCA ES FIGUERAL
This stately farmhouse with swimming pool and many farm animals has been extended a fair few times, now offering eight rooms and suites as well as an apartment sleeping four people. The kitchen uses produce from the farm; you can also request
INSIDER TIP completely vegetarian

South Sea feeling on Mallorca's most beautiful dune beach : Es Trenc

popular items purchased here are the *ensaimadas, cocas* and the home-made chocolates. *Carretera Major | near the church*

WHERE TO STAY

INSIDER TIP AMAPOLA FINCA
Finca hotel with pool and twelve very tastefully furnished suites and rooms; friendly hosts: breakfast is available up to midday! Our tip: the 80 m² Amapola Suite boasts its own pool. *On the country road to sa Rapita*

dishes. *Carretera Campo–Santanyí | at km 42 | tel. 971651641 | www.esfigueral.com | closed Dec–mid-Feb | Moderate*

FINCA SANT BLAI
The four rustic living units of this authentic and cosy country house won't break the bank. If the new swimming pool is not enough, visit the beaches of Colónia de Sant Jordi, some 8 km away. *2 km outside Campos | tel. 971650567 | www.santblai.com | Moderate*

WHERE TO GO

LLUCMAJOR

BALNEARIO SAN JUAN DE LA FONT SANTA (150 B5) *(ﾉﾉ L11)*

After long years of neglect, Mallorca's only hot spring has found a fitting setting in a spa hotel *(19 rooms)* where visitors can enjoy medicinal treatments all year round. *Carretera Campos–Colónia de Sant Jordi | km 8 | tel. 9 71 65 50 16 | www.baleariofontsanta. com | Moderate*

ES TRENC AND PLATJA DE SA RAPITA ★ (150 A4–5) *(ﾉﾉ K11)*

Sample some South Sea feeling on Mallorca, 11 km south of Campos. Unspoilt by buildings, the two natural beaches join seamlessly, making them ideal for extended beach walks. About 5 km long, Es Trenc is considered Mallorca's most beautiful dune beach – which also means of course that in high summer it can be chock-a-block. Since one of the three pay (5.50–10 euros) car parks has had to close, there has been a big issue with parking. Until this is sorted out, it is best to opt for sa Rapita instead and park near the marina.

(149 E4) *(ﾉﾉ J8–9Y)* **Mallorca's fifth-largest municipality (pop. 37,000) has made island history as the place where in 1349 the last Mallorcan king, Jaume III, was killed by the troops of his cousin Pedro IV of Aragon, sealing the fate of the independent kingdom of Mallorca.** A monument on Plaça Espanya commemorates these events. A second monument nearby *(Carrer Bisbe Taxaqet)* praises the town's most important craft: shoemaking. On Wednesdays, Fridays and Sundays the vegetable market on the pretty pedestrianised main square shows what else keeps the inhabitants of Llucmajor busy.

FOOD & DRINK

INSIDER TIP ▶ **CAFÉ COLON**
This village beauty, opened in 1928, has stayed a point of reference thanks to its recent restoration. Locals and foreigners don't wait for market days to enjoy this high-ceilinged and stuccoed townhouse with terrace. *Plaça Espanya 17 | tel. 9 71 66 00 02 | closed Tue and Aug | Budget*

★ **Cabrera**
The boat trip to the protected archipelago lasts about two hours → p. 73

★ **Es Trenc and Platja de Sa Rapita**
The Caribbean on the Mediterranean → p. 67

★ **Capocorb Vell**
Impressive remnants of life 3500 years ago → p. 68

★ **Cala Figuera**
A romantic fishing port attracting many holidaymakers → p. 70

★ **Cala/Parc Natural Mondragó**
Emerald-green swimming coves with protected back country → p. 71

★ **Botanicactus**
An oasis and a desert in a cactus and palm garden → p. 72

MARCO POLO HIGHLIGHTS

LLUCMAJOR

MARRIOTT GOLF RESORT & SPA
Luxury hotel right in the middle of the greens of the two 18-hole golf links of Son Antem East (green fee 69 euros) and West (75 euros) with the largest driving range on the island. The house has three pools and a fabulous spa zone, open to non-residents too (35 euros/day). *150 rooms | Carretera de Llucmajor at km 3.4 | tel. 9 71 12 91 00 | www.marriott.com | Expensive*

SON GALILEU
Rustic finca sleeping two to six people and situated on a large estate, with pool and its own farm. Breakfast and dinner with produce from the farm on request. *6 km south of Llucmajor | tel. 9 71 18 00 29 | www.songalileu.com | Budget–Expensive*

SON GUARDIOLA
This finca with swimming pool and Mallorcan cuisine has a relaxed atmosphere; there are eight rooms and three apartments, each with its own entrance. *Carretera Llucmayor–s'Estanyol, km 2.3 | tel. 9 71 12 12 07 | www.songuardiola.com | Moderate*

CALA BLAVA (148 C4) (*ⱷ G9*)
A clutch of villas some 15 km west of Llucmajor, with a small cliff-fringed cove and places to swimming areas. The *Delta* sports hotel *(288 rooms | tel. 9 71 78 61 35 | www.hdelta.com | Moderate)* is completely geared up towards cyclists, with hire bikes, its own repair service and guided bike tours exploring the surrounding area.

CALA PI (149 D6) (*ⱷ H11*)
In low season, this fjord-like bay 16 km south of town is idyllic. The area above the bay has seen the development of a tasteful *urbanización* with a handful of restaurants.

CAPOCORB VELL ★ (149 D6) (*ⱷ H10*)
Arguably Mallorca's best-preserved Talaiotic settlement, Capocorb Vell dates back to the times around 1400 BC. Prepare to be impressed by the ruined *talaiot* stretching across several levels and the wealth of preserved foundation walls of this residential and defensive complex built from huge stone blocks. *Fri–Wed 10am–4.30pm | admission 2 euros | 12 km south*

Scandinavia on the Mediterranean: the long fjord-like bay of Cala Pi

SANTANYÍ

(150 C4–5) (*M11*) **Surprisingly un-touristy, this tranquil little municipality (pop. 12,000) includes both quiet and lively resorts.**

The homogeneous ensemble with its ochre sandstone houses, pedestrianised zone, and many shops, bars and restaurants makes for a rewarding stroll, particularly on market days *(Wed and Sat)*.

SIGHTSEEING

SANT ANDREU CHURCH

This imposing fortified church from the 18th century houses one of Mallorca's most beautiful historic organs (made by Master Jordi Bosch). In the annual organ weeks it can be heard too. The key is kept opposite at the *rectoría*.

FOOD & DRINK

INSIDER TIP ▶ SA BOTIGA

Café with patio serving breakfast and lunch amidst playful Mediterranean decor. *Next to the church | www.sa-botiga-santanyi.de | open every day | Budget*

The Talaiotic settlement of Capocorb Vell

ES COC

Traditional Mallorcan dishes with a new twist, served with a smile and at fair prices in a pretty town house. Daily set menu 15 and 25 euros. Carrer Aljub 37 | tel. 9 71 64 16 31 | *www.restauran-teescoc.com* | *closed Sun* | *Moderate*

MARKTWIRTSCHAFT/MERCAT

For a change from Mediterranean fare, come here for German culinary staples such as wiener schnitzel, cabbage roulades or curried sausage, cooked by an authentically German chef. On market days the place is packed full. *Plaça Major 6 | www.marktwirtschaft.es | open every day | Moderate*

SANTANYÍ

ALADÍN AND CAMALEÓN
Both shops are under the same management, offering Moorish art, objects and extravagant fashion in the pedestrian zone. *Plaça Major 5*

BOUTIQUE ☺
This little shop on Plaça Major 22 is truly original! Three women make bags, accessories and jewellery, in part from organic wool (fabulously pretty leg warmers made from felt for instance).

LA SAL DE LA VIDA ☺
'The Salt of Life' delicatessen boutique sells *flor de sal*, but also many other organic products from the island. *Carrer Asprer 11*

WHERE TO STAY

SON LLORENC
This small hotel right in the heart of the village of s'Alquería Blanca has named its eight comfortable rooms after Mallorca's winds. Breakfast is enjoyed either in the dining room or in the patio. *Carrer Ramon Llull 7 | tel. 9 71 16 11 61 | www.hotelsonllorenc.com | Moderate–Expensive*

HOTEL SANTANYÍ
This small new town hotel with seven rooms is housed in 300-year-old walls; there is a patio and restaurant too. *Next to the church | tel. 9 71 64 22 14 | www.hotel-santanyi.com | Moderate*

WHERE TO GO

INSIDER TIP CALA DE SA COMUNA/ CALA S'AMUNIA (150 C5) (*ΔΔ M11–12*)
A footpath (about 20 minutes) connects these two natural bays 9 km south of Santanyí. Devoid of any infrastructure, these represent arguably the last beach paradise on Mallorca's eastern coast that is accessible by land. Access to Cala S'Amunia is by a set of steep steps down to the sea (in a bend in the village, to the left of a private house).

CALA FIGUERA ★ (151 D5) (*ΔΔ N11*)
About 5 km southeast of Santanyi, this resort might not have a beach, but instead it is the most idyllic fishing port on the island. On weekdays between 3 and 5pm in particular, the time when the ● INSIDER TIP *fishing boats return to port,* visitors can catch an impressive glimpse of the world of the fishermen. A very good-value and clean accommodation option is the little ☺ *Mar Blau hostal* near the port *(20 rooms | tel. 9 71 64 52 27 | www.marblau.eu)* with a small attached apartment complex, *Vista al Mar (both Budget)*. The Spanish hotel owners' effort to do their bit for sustainable green tourism can be seen in many small details. The *Bon-Bar* with harbour views boasts excellent ice cream sundaes, while *L'Arcada* in the pedestrian zone (but still with sea views) serves fresh fish tapas.

CALA LLOMBARDS (150 C5) (*ΔΔ M11*)
Of the fjord-like bays this one is slightly wider and less heavily frequented; there are no buildings right on the beach. If you're not so keen to spend your money at the overpriced beach bar however, head for the unadorned but much better-value *Sa Torre* bar at the village exit for Mallorcan home cooking.

CALA D'OR/PORTOPETRO (151 D–E4) (*ΔΔ N11*)
Built in the Ibizan style with white-washed houses framed by climbing

flowers, these two holiday resorts 7 km east of Santanyí have nearly merged together now. While Cala d'Or has a perfect tourist infrastructure, the harbour village of Portopetro has preserved a bit of its laid-back character. Cala d'Or has half a dozen small beaches. In terms of hotels, *RIU Cala Esmeralda (151 rooms | tel. 9 71 65 71 11 | Moderate)* right on the bay of the same name has a genteel style; *Rocador (106 rooms | tel. 9 71 65 70 75 | Budget)* lies above Cala Gran. Also on the harbour, the fairly basic *Cafetería La Caracola (tel. 9 71 65 70 13 | open every day | Budget)* serves no-frills regional cuisine. Top-of-the-catch fish and a sumptuous tasting menu with harbour views for 65 euros can be had at *Port Petit (tel. 9 71 64 30 39 | www.portpetit.com | March/April closed Tue | Expensive)*.

CALA/PARC
NATURAL MONDRAGÓ ★
(151 D4–5) (🗺 N11)

This double bay with fine sand and turquoise water owes its protected status to a GOB initiative. There is only sparse housing along the road leading to the bay, which has an information centre for the natural park. At the height of summer it can get very busy here indeed! The neighbouring *Cala S'Amarador* is accessed from Santanyí. *5 km east of Santanyí*

CALA SANTANYÍ (151 D5) (🗺 M11)

Blessed with white sands this pretty bay, situated about 3.5 km south of Santanyí and great for swimming, is fringed by some hotels and summer houses. The recently renovated hotel *Cala Santanyí* directly on the bay has 24 rooms and 28 apartments. Clean and tidy, this is a very family-friendly choice *(tel. 9 71 16 55 05 | www.hotelcalasantanyi. com | Moderate)*.

Fun in the sun, swimming at Cala Figuera

ORATORI DE LA CONSOLACIÓ ☀
(151 D4) (🗺 M10)

Atop the Puig Gros at the southern end of the Serra de Llevant, some 4 km northeast of Santanyí, a small 16th-century church houses the 'rainmaker' Virgin Mary, the *Mare de Déu de la Consolació*. The a church terrace affords magnificent and far-reaching views towards the sea.

SES SALINES

(150 B5) (🗺 L11) Once a sleepy village, Ses Salines (pop. 5100 including all the surrounding farms) at the very bottom of the hot south has awakened from its Sleeping Beauty slumber.

The town benefits from its golden sandy beaches – some of which are protected – and the hotel resort of Colònia de Sant Jordi, as well as from the salt lakes. The huge *s'Avall* estate belonging to the March banking family also forms part of the municipality. Today, some good restaurants and shops have opened up along the thoroughfare.

SIGHTSEEING

BOTANICACTUS ⭐

With over 1000 types of cacti from all over the world, and an extensive Mediterranean habitat, the complex, covering 5000 m², claims to be Europe's largest botanical gardens. What is certainly true is that since its opening in 1989, the garden with its artificial lake and restaurant become a refreshing oasis in the hot south. *At the exit of the village going in the direction of Santanyí (Ma6100) | in winter 10.30am–4.30pm | summer 9am–6.30pm | admission 7 euros*

FOOD & DRINK

INSIDER TIP ▶ ASADOR ES TEATRE

Right next to his famous fish restaurant, Manolo and his partners have worked their magic to convert a theatre into a grill restaurant – completely decked out in burgundy red. There's also a terrace. Thanks to a special method of slow-cooking pork and lamb for six to seven hours, the meat has much less fat! Daily set menu 10 and 15 euros. The place also doubles up as an art gallery, wine bodega and gift shop. *Next to Casa Manolo | tel. 9 71 64 95 40 | www.asado resteatre. com | closed Tue | Moderate*

CASA MANOLO (BODEGA BARAHONA)

It's not so much tapas that have elevated this cosy and authentic small eatery into the ranks of the best fish restaurants, but the excellently grilled fresh fish and seafood. Many VIPs come to eat here, led by Crown Prince Felipe and Leticia. Our tip for your first course: choose the INSIDER TIP ▶ *Calamares en su tinta* prepared by Manolo himself at your table. Last not least: a reservation is a must! *At the church | tel. 9 71 64 91 30 | www. bodegabarahona.com | closed Mon | Moderate–Expensive*

WHERE TO STAY

INSIDER TIP ▶ CAN BONICO

2009 saw the opening of this fancy new hotel, converted from a 13th-century manor house right in the heart of the village. The 28 classy rooms and suites are resplendently white on white with just a few dots of colour. There's also a swimming pool and a good restaurant with terrace. *Carrer Sant Bartomeu 8 | tel. 9 71 64 90 22 | www.hotel canbonico. com | Moderate–Expensive*

WHERE TO GO

COLÒNIA DE SANT JORDI (150 A5) (*ΩΩ K11*)

Particularly pretty it ain't, this hub of tourist accommodation and second

LOW BUDGET

▶ A guided tour through Llucmajor also tells part of fascinating island history, especially enjoyable when told with a personal touch as by Matías Tomás Cardell, free of charge. *Variable dates | booking tel. 9 71 44 10 71*

▶ For only 16 euros, even non-residents can use the thermal spa pool of San Juan – a good-value alternative to the expensive spas!

Casa Manolo: the place to enjoy wonderfully tasty seafood and fish dishes

homes 5.5 km south of Ses Salines. However, in recent years, efforts have been made to give some structure to the settlement with pedestrianised promenades and green spaces. The colourful little harbour provides a romantic touch; this is the starting point for walks to the unspoilt beaches of *Es Dolç* and the dream beaches of *Es Carbó* and *ses Roquetes* further to the southeast. The *Es Turó* guesthouse *(16 rooms | tel. 9 71 65 50 57 | Budget)* with a pretty terrace restaurant overlooking the harbour is at the edge of town. The well-run *Don León* hotel *(116 rooms, 10 suites | tel. 9 71 65 55 61 | www. hoteldonleon.com | Expensive)* is located on the cliff-lined coast with access to the sea. The port is the starting point for charming day trips by boat to ★ ☺ *Cabrera,* the protected archipelago which can be glimpsed from the shore, boasting a castle and interesting endemic flora and fauna *(April–Oct daily 9.30am | tel. 9 71 64 90 34).* The excursion costs 38 euros *(add 7 euros to include lunch)* and includes a swim in the Blue Grotto – memories for some maybe of Capri? – and a guided tour of the castle.

SALINES DE LLEVANT ☺
(140 A4–5) *(⌖ X–X Y-Y)*

Every year the managers of this private saline works measuring just under 1.5 km² extract 8000 tons of table salt. Even if the saline works themselves are fenced in and not open to visitors, it's worth having a look at the white mountains of salt piled up to dry. Katja Wöhr from Switzerland has rented over 80 of the seawater basins to harvest **INSIDER TIP** *flor de sal* for her delicacies, which these days are sold worldwide, in her shop in Santanyi and now also directly at the salt works in her slightly bohemian-style **INSIDER TIP** delicatessen boutique with café.

The surrounding strictly protected saline lakes of *es Salobrar,* best seen by cycling around them, are home to nearly 170 species of birds. *9 km south of Campos*

THE CENTRE

Es Plá, 'the plain', is what they call the centre of the island. The rural depopulation suffered by this strongly agricultural region has left its mark to this day. At the beginning of the 1970s, Mallorca's former cereal basket entered a crisis, which the locals have since attempted to counter with new farming methods and a return to traditional ways of making a living, such as viniculture and crafts.

The late 1980s saw the appearance of the magic words *agroturisme* and *turismo rural*, turning many a local farmer into a part-time hotelier. The softly undulating landscape is criss-crossed by narrow tarmac roads connecting all villages. This is an area for discovering disused wells, pretty wayside crosses and vicar-ages, as well as chapels, hermitages and monasteries. Whilst the now widened Ma15 from Palma to Manacor has to contend with a lot of traffic, it still qualifies as a picturesque holiday road, serving rewarding destinations such as Algaida, Montuïri and Vilafranca along the way.

ALGAIDA

(149 E2) (*JZ J7*) The first thing both locals and tourists notice in the Plá's largest municipality (pop. 4500) is the number of restaurants along the Ma15: it is not for nothing that Algaida is known as 'foodie town'.

The restaurants serve good Mallorcan cuisine in an old tradition: stagecoaches

A fertile plain and gentle hills:
a chance to experience Mallorcan day-to-day
life off the beaten tourist track

once stopped here. The town itself is rather unspectacular.

SIGHTSEEING

VIDRIOS GORDIOLA ●

The island's oldest glass-blowing establishment has been going since 1719; it can be found at the westerly exit leaving town, on the Ma15 at kilometre 19. You can watch the glass blowers at work, and admire old and new pieces, in the attached small glass museum. *Daily except Sun 9am–7pm*

FOOD & DRINK

CAL DIMONI

Huge, rustic and very Mallorcan: this is a veteran amongst Algaida's eateries. On a Sunday though it often gets horrendously busy! | *On the Ma15 at km 21* | *tel. 9 71 66 50 35* | *closed Wed* | *Moderate*

HOSTAL D'ALGAIDA

Cosy restaurant-cum-shop selling its own products, regional cuisine, good ambiance with a counter groaning under the

The Santuari de Nostra Senyora de Gràcia is one of Puig de Randa's three monasteries

wealth of home-made island produce. This is the place to try ● *pa amb oli*! *Ma15 at km 21 | tel. 9 71 66 51 09 | open every day* | *Moderate*

APARTAMENTS RURALS RAIMS
Manor house with picturesque patio and pool, offering one suite and four apartments on the edge of town; dinner for residents. *Carrer Ribera 24 | tel. 9 71 66 51 57 | www.finca-raims.com* | *Moderate–Expensive*

WHERE TO GO

PUIG DE RANDA ★ (149 E3) (ⓜ *J8*)
At 542m, Mallorca's only table mountain is the highest elevation on the Plá. It is worth strolling through the cobbled alleyways in the village of *Randa* (pop. 100), which sits at the foot of the mountain. Above Randa, the mountain road leads first of all to the ☀ *Santuari de Nostra Senyora de Gràcia,* the lowest of three monasteries. The abandoned 15th-century hermitage with sweeping views across the plain from Llucmajor to the archipelago of Cabrera has been restored, the sandstone rock stabilised, and parking spaces made available. About 1 km uphill, the *Santuari de Sant Honorat* was founded at the end of the 14th century and is inhabited by monks to this day. The only part that is accessible is the 17th-century chapel. At first glimpse, the anticipated 'wow' factor of the ascent is lessened somewhat by radar masts on the hilltop, but the sweeping views from the ☀ terrace of the *Santuari de Nostra Senyora de Cura* at the summit more than make up for it. In terms of cultural history, the last-named is the most important of the three monasteries. In 1263, the Santuari was the chosen retreat of Ramón Llull after he gave up his hedonistic life at the Mallorcan court. In

all, Llull wrote 265 works, most of them in Catalan, elevating it to a language of literature. He researched, taught and proselytised all over the world. 'Love makes the independent its servant and gives slaves freedom': This Llull quote – immortalised on his monument in Palma – speaks for the open-minded spirit of this great thinker and missionary.

Today, the classroom where grammar was taught in the old school of Cura on the mountain houses a *Ramón Llull Museum (Tue–Sun 11am–1pm and 4–6pm)*. Make sure you try the INSIDERTIP *Licor Randa*, a herbal liqueur which you can only get up here! The simple option for staying overnight and getting something to eat is one of the 26 former monastery cells *(tel. 9 71 12 02 60 | Budget)*. For more creature comforts, choose the *Es Recó de Randa* hotel *(28 rooms and suites | tel. 9 71 66 09 97 | www.esrecoderanda.com | Expensive)* at the foot of the mountain, with spectacular views from the ☙ terrace. A swimming pool and a fine Mallorcan restaurant are all part of the package. *4 km south of Algaida*

MONTUÏRI

(149 F2) (*⌖ K7*) With its sturdy parish church and 19 mill towers, testimonies to a long agricultural tradition, this stretched-out hilltop village (pop. 2300) of Arabic origin is pretty as a picture.

Today, the small town owes its fame to breeding partridges and to the fact that in 1995 the famous *Perlas Orquídeas* pearl company transferred one of its factories here. A stroll around the *plaça* (with the weekly market on a Monday) leads past well-preserved houses, wells, wayside crosses and mills, as well as past the broad flight of steps in front of the parish church of *Sant Bartomeu*, dating back to

the 16th to 18th centuries. In the town hall awaits a ready-made alternative to beach tourism: a one-hour stroll INSIDERTIP to the town's most beautiful windmills, with an introduction to the history of grain milling from the second century BC onwards.

FOOD & DRINK

SON BASCÓS
A simple grill restaurant for day visitors has been added to this quail and partridge farm. Quail eggs form the appetiser, followed by grilled *guàtleres* and *perdius*. *Near Ma15, at km 29 (signposted) | closed Tue and lunchtime (except Sun) | tel. 9 71 64 61 70 | Budget*

WHERE TO STAY

ES PUIG MOLTÓ ☙
18 picture-perfect rooms, suites and apartments in a restored estate with pool and a magnificent view across the surrounding farmland. *Carretera Pina–*

★ **Puig de Randa**
Dream views from Mallorca's only table mountain → p. 76

★ **Els Calderés**
Deep insights into the feudal way of life on the estate in the olden days, for young and old → p. 78

★ **Ermita de Bonany**
Meet a peasant Madonna and enjoy sweeping views across the heart of the island → p. 79

★ **Sineu animal market**
Now every Wednesday: 700-year-old market → p. 80

MARCO POLO HIGHLIGHTS

Montuïri at km 3 | tel. 9 71 18 17 58 | www.espuigmolto.com | Expensive

PETRA

WHERE TO GO

ELS CALDERÉS ★ ● (145 F5) (*M L7*)

The fortification-like manor house, built around 1700, with its own chapel, wine cellar, stables, servants' quarters and aristocratic salons, conveys an idea of former feudal life. The most impressive feature is the huge larder with harvested crops. *7 km east at Sant Joan on the Ma15, km 37 (signposted) | daily 10am–6pm | admission 7 euros*

PORRERES (145 E6) (*M L8*)

A widening of the approach roads has made this small town 7 km south of Montuï (pop. 5300) more accessible. The weekly market on a Tuesday makes the ideal excuse for a visit, as it is only on that day *(10.30am–12.30pm)* that the town hall *(Casa de Vila)* opens its remarkable exhibition of around 300 objects of contemporary art (amongst them two Dalís). The rose window and bell tower of the parish church on the market square are impressive too. Right next to the church, the *Centre (tel. 9 71 16 83 72 | open every day | Budget)*, a former theatre, today functions as a rustic restaurant with down-to-earth fare. The rural hotel complex of *Sa Bassa Rotja (Camino Sa Pedrera | tel. 9 71 16 82 25 | www.sabassarotja.com | Expensive)* with 25 luxury suites, two pools, beauty farm and restaurant lies outside the town. These days, Porreres has returned to making a living from its wine. Right in the heart of the town, for instance, you can visit the organic ☺ ● bodega *Jaume Mesquida (Carrer Vileta 7 | tel. 9 71 64 71 06 | by appointment at www.jaumemesquida.com)* of island-wide fame. This vineyard no longer uses chemical pesticides or fertilisers.

(146 A4) (*M M6–7*) **The alleyways of this sleepy village (pop. 2700) were laid out in their chequer-board pattern under Jaume I.**

Petra was called 'The Luminous One' by its Arabic founders in an allusion to its Jordanian sister. Petra's second great claim to fame is its most famous son, Fra ● Juníper Serra, Franciscan monk and missionary. From 1769 onwards Serra founded 21 mission stations in California, which were to develop into cities with millions of inhabitants, such as San Francisco and Los Angeles.

SIGHTSEEING

CASA NATAL I MUSEU JUNÍPER SERRA

Find out the story of the life of the missionary (1713–84) in the house of his birth, today functioning as a museum. *Carrer Barracar/Carrer Fra Juníper Serra | tel. for making an appointment 9 71 56 11 49 | key kept at Carrer Miguel de Petra, 2, to the right of the museum | free, donations appreciated*

BODEGA MIQUEL OLIVIER

With this bodega Petra can boast one of the most famous on the island. Today, daughter Pilar Olivier rules the roost as enologist and cellar mistress. Her dry Muscat has been crowned the best white wine in Spain. *Carrer Font 26 (signposted) | www.miqueloliver.com*

FOOD & DRINK WHERE TO STAY

ES CELLER

There's no place quite as cosily old-fashioned and with such unique ambiance as this cellar tavern right in the heart of the town. The quality of the dishes unfortunately oscillates between excellent and mediocre. *Carrer de l'Hospital 46 | (signposted) | tel. 9 71 56 10 56 | closed Mon | Budget*

SA PLAÇA PETRA

The tiny village hotel, with its lovingly decorated restaurant and inviting patio, is worth a visit, and the three pretty rooms are let at a fair price. The nicely presented menu however doesn't quite live up to its promises. *Plaça Ramón Llull 4 | tel. 9 71 56 16 46 | Moderate*

WHERE TO GO

ARIANY (146 A3) (⨂ M6)

This small village (pop. 920) 2.5 km north of Petra only achieved independence from its neighbour in 1982. The village's heart is its church, whose dreamy ⋇ front garden, full of blooms and boasting sweeping views, is well worth a stop for taking a breather. The restaurant *Ses Torres (open every day | Budget)* at the big roundabout just outside Ariany is a huge pit stop for truck drivers and day trippers where you can get good tapas and a good-value set meal.

ERMITA DE BONANY ★ ⋇
(146 A5) (⨂ L7)

A detour to the monastery is worth doing for the chubby-faced Madonna figure dating back to the 8th century and the panoramic view alone. The monastery owes its name (Good Year) to the end of a period of severe drought. At the entrance, tiled images are a reminder of the long-awaited rain and the rich harvest that followed. There is also a fantastic picnic area with tables and benches under a canopy of shade-giving trees – contributing to the 'end of the world' feel here. *4 km south of Petra*

SENCELLES

(144 145 C–D4) (⨂ J6) **The charm of this region to the west of the Plà lies in the many hamlets surrounding Sencelles, all well restored, all pretty to behold.**

The magnificent altar in the Ermita de Bonany

In Sencelles itself (pop. 2700), the village at the heart of all the others, the traditions of making bagpipes and of cultivating figs have been preserved to this day. However, the village has now become first and foremost a choice spot for foreigners' second homes.

FOOD & DRINK

CELLER SON ALOY ⋇

Restaurant on the summit of a vineyard serving fabulous T-bone and rib-eye steaks straight off the charcoal grill. *Carretera Sencelles–Inca at km 3 | tel. 9 71 88 38 24 | open every day | Moderate*

WHERE TO STAY

SA TORRE
The friendly owners of this 300-year-old rural estate offer six units to choose from, with two pools, in the hamlet *Ses Alqueríes*, 2 km away. The four-course **INSIDER TIP** tasting menu for 39 euros is served in the property's prettiest room: its wine cellar, with walls 10 metres high; it feels like eating on a film set. *Tel. 9 71 14 40 11 | www.sa-torre.com | closed Mon | Expensive*

WHERE TO GO

COSTITX (145 D3) (*Ø K6*)
Situated 4.5 km further east in a pretty position on a hill, the village (pop. 1000) was made famous by the find, in 1894, of three bronze bull heads dating back to Talaiotic times. The pieces are exhibited in the

LOW BUDGET

▶ A good-value means of transport is the train (SFM), especially as its network has been extended over the past few years. Alongside the historic line connecting Palma and Sóller, trains now also run between Palma, Inca and Manacor, with stops of interest to tourists such as Sinéu, Petra, sa Pobla and Muro along the way. A Palma–Manacor return trip for instance costs 3.60 euros.

▶ Of interest to the entire family and free to boot is watching glass blowers at work at *Gordiola* near Algaida. A visit to the museum, which tells the story of one of the oldest crafts on the island, is free, too. *Workshop Mon–Sat 9am–1.30pm and 3–6pm*

Museu de Ciències in the *Casal de Cultura* (at the village entrance coming from Sencelles | Tue–Fri 9am–1pm | admission 3 euros). Near Costitx you can also find the Balearics' only observatory, in existence since 1991; it serves research purposes, but also offers amateur astronomy classes in Spanish, *by appointment, tel. 6 50 38 68 81.* In the **INSIDER TIP** planetarium next door *(www.mallorcaplanetarium.com)* visitors can experience over 6000 virtual stars and may view the real thing through telescopes. A replica of the Apollo 11 spacecraft is also on view *(Fri/Sat 8pm | admission 10 euros).*

SINEU

(145 E3–4) (*Ø K–L6*) **Of all the villages in the centre of the island, Sineu (pop. 3400) is the most famous. This is mainly due to the ★ *animal market of Sineu* every Wednesday, which has been held here since 1306 and is the largest of its kind in Mallorca.**

The best time to visit the market is very early in the morning, before the tourist buses arrive. But there is much more to Sineu than just the market: of Talaiotic-Roman origin and later one of the island's six main Arabic settlements, in medieval times Sineu was chosen by King Jaume II as his residence.

SIGHTSEEING

CENTRE D'ART S'ESTACIÓ
Contemporary Mallorcan art is shown in the restored Art Nouveau train station, which only exhibits works produced on the island. *Mon–Fri 9.30am–2pm and 4–7pm | www.sineuestacio.com*

MARE DE DEU DELS ANGELS
A broad flight of steps leads up to the massive church, which reveals a surpris-

ingly delicate-looking interior. A winged bronze lion, symbol of St Mark, patron saint of Sineu, guards the church with its 16th-century statue of the Virgin. The *Casa Rectoral* (rectory) exhibits nearly 800 ceramics dating back to the 12th and 13th centuries *(Wed at market times or by appointment | tel. 9 71 52 00 40)*.

a great choice for romantic souls. *Next to the church in the neighbouring village of Llubí | 7 km | tel. 9 71 85 71 38 | www. canperico.com | Budget–Moderate*

LEÓN DE SINEU

Historic townhouse with eight rooms, a garden, pool and wine cellar. The in-

Animals have been bought and sold at Sineu market for over 700 years

FOOD & DRINK

CELLER ES GROP

Small and cosy, with friendly service. *Carrer Major 18 | (pedestrian area) | tel. 9 71 52 01 87 | Sun evening and Mon | Budget*

CELLER SON TOREO

Less romantic, but very authentic, and incredibly popular with the locals. *Carrer Son Torelló 1 | tel. 9 71 52 01 38 | closed Mon | Budget*

WHERE TO STAY

CAN PERICÓ

With only three rooms, a good restaurant and a pretty courtyard, this small but perfectly formed hotel **INSIDER TIP** is

house *sa Boveda* restaurant serves a daily set meal, and on Saturday evenings lays on a barbecue. *Carrer dels Bous 129 | tel. 9 71 52 02 11 | www.hotel-leondesineu. com | Moderate–Expensive*

WHERE TO GO

S'OLIERA DE SON CATIU

(145 E3) (*Ø K6*)

The new, state-of-the-art *tafona* (oil mill) 12 km northwest of Sineu with a large restaurant *(excellent pa amb olis!)* and sale of Mallorcan products is well worth visiting. In early October, farmers and finca owners bring in olives by the sackful. Ask staff to show you how the olives are processed, and the machines. *Carretera Llubí–Inca at the roundabout (Carretera Muro) | www.soncatiu.com*

PALMA AND THE WEST

The southwest of the island is dominated by the capital, Palma de Mallorca. With just over 400,000 inhabitants Palma represents over a third of the island's population; this is also where all Mallorca's main roads converge.

About two thirds of the island's overall 270,000 hotel beds are spread along the broad bay of Badía de Palma and in the coastal resorts between the capital and Sant Elm out west. You won't find worse urban spread along the coast. On the other hand, nor will you find a better infrastructure. Despite all the urban development the hilly back country has managed to hang on to much of its scenic beauty.

PALMA

▨▨▨ **MAP INSIDE BACK COVER**
▨▨▨ (143 E–F4) (*∅ E–F 7*) One of the things that makes Palma so fascinating to both locals and foreigners is that this town is both old and young.

Everything is close together here: the peaceful courtyards of splendid aristocratic palaces and street cafés seemingly stranded in heavy traffic; contemplative dark church interiors heavy with incense and busy action in the bright lights of the covered market halls; squares baking in the sun and shady arcades. Visitors should really look to explore the town on foot. For one, the streets of the Old Town are narrow and

Mallorca's heart beats down on the left-hand side of the island, with the prettiest town in the Mediterranean and the top tourist resorts in the west

CITY

WHERE TO START?
(U C6) (⟁ c4) Car: car park on Parc de la Mar. Then walk: cathedral, upper Old Town, Plaça Cort, Plaça Major, Mercat d'Olivar, Plaça Espanya, lower Old Town, Born, Llotja, harbour. Bus: bus station on Plaça Espanya. Tour taking in Mercat d'Olivar, Plaças Major and Cort, cathedral, Palau March, lower Old Town, harbour, Llotja, Born.

follow a complicated one-way system, for another the expensive ORA parking control system, allowing only up to an hour and a half, severely limits sightseeing time. If you want a space in one of Palma's multistorey car parks, take your vehicle there in the early morning, as afterwards the city with the highest traffic density in Spain becomes chock-a-block. A much better idea is to join an expertly led **INSIDER TIP** 'Stroll through History'; for more information, check the boxed text on page 93.

SIGHTSEEING

BANYS ARABS/ARC DE S'ALMUDAINA ●
(U D5–6) (*Ⓜ d5–6*)

Arabic baths – well, strictly speaking, the plural is wrong, as all that is left to see is a dome and pillars with various 10th-century capitals. The gardens are a good spot for relaxation; gardens and baths

castle dominates the town. Begun under Jaume I and completed in 1309, it served only briefly as a residence for Jaume II, later as a dungeon and a place of terrible pogroms against the Jewish population (14th century). Today, the castle houses the historical museum. The courtyard is used for concerts. The view of the city and port alone makes the drive up worth-

The Fundació Pilar i Joan Miró shows works by the modernist artist

belong to the *Font i Roig* palace, connected by a bridge. *Carrer Can Serra 7 | daily 9.30am–6pm, in summer to 8pm | admission 2 euros*

ES BALUARD ★ (U A4) (*Ⓜ a4*)

This modern building fits in brilliantly with Palma's historic fortifications, forming a fascinating contrast to the contemporary Spanish and international artworks. Great views of port and cathedral can be had from the 🔆 INSIDERTIP roof terraces. *Plaça Porta de Santa Catalina | Tue–Sun 10am–9pm (in winter 10am–8pm) | www.esbaluard.org | admission 6 euros, free on public holidays (informative English-language audio guide)*

CASTELL DE BELLVER 🔆
(143 E4) (*Ⓜ E7*)

Sturdy and defensive from the outside, rather elegant in its circular interior courtyard framed by loggias, the royal

while. *April–Sept Mon–Sat 8am–8.30pm, Sun 10am–6.30pm, Oct–March Mon–Sat 8am–7pm, Sun 10am–4.30pm | admission 2.50 euros, Sun free*

CONVENT DE SANT FRANCESC
(U E5) (*Ⓜ e5*)

The highlights of the otherwise fairly sober church facade are the rose window and the Baroque portal. The interior of the large 17th-century basilica shelters a magnificent Baroque altar, as well as the tomb of philosopher and missionary Ramón Llull. The monastery building with its beautiful Gothic cloisters is home to a school. *Plaça Sant Francesc | Mon–Sat 9.30am–12.30pm and 3.30–6pm, Sun 9.30am–12.30pm | admission 1 euro*

FUNDACIÓ PILAR I JOAN MIRÓ ★
(143 E4) (*Ⓜ e4*)

Following the wishes of Joan Miró (1893–1983), a Catalan by birth and a

Mallorcan by choice who worked for 40 years on the island, the artist's studio and residence were converted into a 'place where people live, create and talk together'. Part of Miró's bequest can be seen in the museum building; there are also changing exhibitions of artists who share a similar artistic language. At certain times, Miró's studio and the *Son Boter* house are also open to visits. *Cala Major | Carrer Saridakis 29 (signposted) | Tue–Sat in summer 10am–7pm, in winter 10am–6pm, Sun 10am–3pm | admission 6 euros*

ART NOUVEAU BUILDINGS

In Palma some beautifully restored facades show the Catalan version of Art Nouveau, *modernisme*. To name but a few: *Edifici Casayas* on Plaça Mercat, built in 1908–11 by Francesc Roca. Diagonally opposite, on Plaça Weyler, arguably the city's most beautiful Art Nouveau facade: the ★ *Gran Hotel,* built in 1901–03 by Lluís Domenec i Montaner, extensively restored by a bank and converted into an art gallery with restaurant *(Tue–Sat 10am–9pm, Sun 10am–2pm).* Standing

Art Nouveau at the Gran Hotel

next to each other on the Plaça Marqués de Palmer, the houses *Can Rei* and *L'Aguila* were built in 1908–09 and are famous for their colourful mosaics. It is here that the influence of the great master of Catalan *modernisme*, Antoni Gaudí, makes itself felt the most. In contrast, *Can Corbella* in Carrer Jaume II shows Moorish influence.

LA SEU CATHEDRAL ★ (U C6) *(⌂ c4)*

The most famous building on the island seems to sit above the sea not unlike a protective mother hen. From the outside, the ● church doesn't begin to convey the height and light it displays inside. The main nave, some 110 m long, boasts 14 slim pillars, just under 22 m high and the large rose window in the main apse (11.5 m in diameter), made up from 1236 pieces of glass, transforms the rays of the sun into a colourful spectacle. Another enchanting sight is the Gaudí chandelier above the altar – and the **INSIDER TIP** 'Feeding of the 5000' in St Peter's Chapel, a giant ceramic work by the Mallorcan artist Miquel Barceló. *Plaça Palau Reial | Mon–Fri June–Sept 10am–6.15pm, April–May and Oct 10am–5.15pm, Nov–March 10am–3.15pm, Sat 10am–2.15pm | admission 4 euros*

MUSEU DE MALLORCA ●
(U C–D6) *(⌂ d6)*

This 17th-century town palace exhibits some 3000 items from the island's prehistory to the Baroque period, archaeological finds as well as paintings, sculptures, furniture and sacred art; there is a pretty courtyard too. *Carrer Sa Portella 5 | April–Sept Tue–Sat 10am–7pm, Oct–March 10am–1pm and 4–6pm, Sun 10am–2pm | free of charge*

PALAUS (PALACES)

Most of the palaces of the local bourgeoisie and nobility, usually erected in the 15th and 16th centuries in the Italian style, can be found in the Old Town around the cathedral and in Sa Portella.

Spacious square framed by arcaded houses: Plaça Major

These buildings are characterised by sober, fortress-like facades and cheerful patios. The palaces are normally not open to the public. However, some allow the occasional glimpse through iron grilles of the cobblestoned patios with flower-bedecked fountains. Particularly beautiful is the *Palau Marqués* in *Carrer Zanglada 2 | (Mon–Sat 10am–3pm | admission 6 euros)*. Easy to visit and free: *Casal Solleric* on *Passeig des Born 27 (Tue–Sat 10am–2pm and 5–9pm, Sun 10am–1.30pm)* which has been converted into an art gallery and café. The best time to visit the palaces is INSIDERTIP► the week around Corpus Christi (a moveable feast) where about a third of the overall 154 town palaces open their patio. Some of them put on concerts at that time too *(for more information, check with the tourist offices)*.

PALAU MARCH MUSEU
(U B–C5) (*m b–c5*)

In 2003, the descendants of island legend Joan March opened their town pal-

ace to the public, to display an impressive collection of art works, amongst them a ● Neapolitan nativity scene with over 1000 figures and other parts. The ground floor houses a pretty branch of the 'Cappuccino' chain of coffee houses. *Carrer Palau Reial 18 | Mon–Fri 10am–6.30pm (in winter 10am–6pm), Sat 10am–2pm | admission 3.60 euros*

PALAU DE S'ALMUDAINA
(U C 5–6) (*m c5–6*)

Seen from the sea, the cathedral and the royal palace appear like one and the same building. The former alcázar – a Moorish castle – of the emir, later a residence of the Aragonese kings, today houses the military headquarters and accommodates King Juan Carlos I when he spends time in Mallorca. The highlights of the palace are the royal chambers and the Gothic chapel of Santa Ana. *Carrer Palau Reial | in winter Mon–Fri 10am–2pm and 4–6pm, in summer 10am–6.30pm, Sat 10am–2pm | admission 3.20 euros, with guided tour 4 euros*

PLAÇAS (SQUARES)

Just sit down and look around with a cup of coffee or a glass of wine: this is the favourite pastime of locals and visitors alike on Palma's squares, such as the *Plaça de Cort* (U D5) (*m d5*), the pedestrianised town hall square with the olive tree that has been standing here in front of the *ajuntament* for several hundred years. Or take the stock-exchange square *Plaça Llotja* (U B5) (*m b5*), with views of the former maritime stock exchange dating from the 15th century (today used as an exhibition space) and the port. The pretty rectangular *Plaça Major* (U D4) (*m d4*), the main square in the upper town, seamlessly framed by yellow-painted facades of houses and arcades, is almost completely in the hands of tourists. It's a different story in the cafés on the *Plaça Espanya* (U E2) *(ⅲ e2)*; here, the locals tend to be left to themselves. In a swirl of pigeons Jaume I looks down from his pedestal onto this busy transport hub with the bus station and terminus of the Sóller railway. Around the corner, housewives and foodies meet at *Plaça de*

CENTRO CULTURAL SES VOLTES
(U C6) *(ⅲ c6)*

In the cultural centre in the city wall south-east of the cathedral, visible from the path along the city wall, changing art exhibitions are held, and in the courtyard avant-garde concerts are sometimes held. *Parc de la Mar | May–Oct Tue–Sat 10am–1pm*

These days, it's no longer just fishing boats: the port of Palma

l'Olivar (U E3) *(ⅲ e3)*, before or after the shopping in the *mercat,* the town's largest market hall – not without trying some tapas in the **INSIDER TIP** *Bar d'es Peix* in the fishmarket hall *(Mon–Sat to 2pm).* The place where everybody fetches up at one stage or another is the *Plaça Rei Joan Carles* (U C4) *(ⅲ c4)* with a turtle obelisk in its centre, *Bar Bosch* and *Café Solleric.*

PORT (U A–B 5–6) *(ⅲ a–b 5–6)*
The fishing port is limited by the long jetty reaching out into the sea below the cathedral. This is also where the ships leave for the one-hour ● *Cruceros Marco Polo* cruises around the harbour *(Mon–Sat hourly between 11am and 4pm | 10 euros per person);* a refreshing and relaxing change for visitors whose feet need a break.

and 5–8.45 pm | free admission

FOOD & DRINK

The **INSIDER TIP** *Carrer Fábrica* in the Santa Catalina quarter has developed into the town's 'food mile', one kilometre long. Mainly it's locals who frequented this leafy street with its countless pubs and restaurants. Don't bother turning up before 9pm, or you'll only have your own company! Very popular for its imaginative small Mediterranean platters (there is no printed menu) is the *Fábrica 23* bistro *(tel. 9 71 45 31 25 | closed Sun–Mon | Budget)*, now in *Carrer Cotoner 42.* Table reservations are a must! A promising newcomer is *Duke, Carrer Soler 36 (Budget)* with decoration as exotic as the menu.

BAR BOSCH (U C3) (*ᗰ c3*)

There is no way round this city meeting point, as evidenced by the noise and scrum. Make sure to try *langostas* (warm bread rolls with *jamon serrano*)! *Plaça de Rei Joan Carles*

LA BÓVEDA (U B5) (*ᗰ b5*)

Popular and well-established tapas restaurant with a rustic atmosphere. *Carrer Sa Portería 2 | from 1.30pm and 8.30pm onwards, closed Sun | Moderate*

GRAN CAFÉ CAPPUCCINO
(U C3, D5) (*ᗰ c3, d5*)

A coffee-house chain which still manages to be a hip hangout in a restored *palacio* in *Carrer Sant Miquel, 53, near Plaça Espanya, in Palau March and on Passeig Marítim 1*

INSIDER TIP 13 % (U B3) (*ᗰ b3*)

This lower ground floor eatery offers good food and good value. Fresh colours dominate the decor, the small Mediterranean dishes are tasty. Set lunch menu! *Carrer Feliu 13 | (a side street of Passeig des Born) | closed Sun | Budget*

ES MOLLET (143 F4) (*ᗰ F7*)

A gifted chef magics up the most wonderful grilled fish, to be enjoyed with views of the small port of Es Molinar/Portixol in the east of Palma – at fairytale prices however. *tel. 9 71 24 71 09 | closed Sun | Expensive*

NAUTIC (143 E4) (*ᗰ E8*)

Fine dining with unbeatable views of port and cathedral. Enjoy fabulous fish dishes, such as the *Noches del Mar* set menu, costing 45 euros including wine. *Muelle de San Pedro 1 | tel. 9 71 72 63 83 | www.nautic-restaurant.com | closed Sun | Expensive*

SIMPLY FOSH ☺ (U D3) (*ᗰ d3*)

Slow Food chef Marc Fosh and his team use seasonal products to create stunning dishes that are anything but simple, and serve them in their patio restaurant in the exclusive Convent de la Missió hotel, decorated in light and fresh colours. The three-course **INSIDER TIP** set lunch menu costs only 18 euros. *Carrer Missió 7a | tel. 9 71 72 01 14 | www.simplyfosh.com | closed Sun | Moderate–Expensive*

TRAS (U C4) (*ᗰ c4*)

New, fresh-looking bistro serving tapas and *pinchos,* warm and cold mini snacks which are charged by the number of toothpicks used to spear the delicious tidbits. The friendly service makes a welcome contrast to the two long-established Lizarrán eateries. *Carrer Unió 2 | open every day | Budget*

LOW BUDGET

► Travellers wanting to save the admission charge at Palma's La Seu Cathedral may enter at Mass for free, but have to refrain from walking around. *Sun and public holidays 9am, midday, 1pm, 7pm, on weekdays 9am*

► In the well-kept 93-bed youth hostel on Platja de Palma travellers under 25 pay only 12.40 euros per night, those over 25 still only 13.27 euros. *Carrer Costa -Brava 13 | tel. (*) 9 02 11 11 88*

► A night at the Hostal Apuntadores right in the vibrant Llotja quarter costs only 50 euros; a fabulous roof terrace makes up for the lack of breakfast. *Carrer Apuntadores 8 | tel. 9 71 71 34 91 | www.palmahostales.com*

VERD I BLAU (U D1) *(ω d1)*

Decorated in shades of green and blue, this restaurant with patio takes an eco-friendly attitude, spoiling its guests with Mediterranean cooking using lots of fresh produce at excellent value for money. *Carrer 31 de Dicembre 9 | tel. 9 71 29 80 63 | closed Sun and public holidays | Moderate*

SHOPPING

INSIDER TIP BUNYOLS BONÍSSIMS (U D4) *(ω d4)*

Watch typical Mallorcan potato fritters in the shape of a doughnut being made – and try them of course. Four euros will buy you 250 g. *Carrer Sant Miguel opposite the church of Sant Antoni*

CENTRE DE MODA (U C3) *(ω c3)*

Fashion designer Tolo Crespí and hair stylist Carlos Martín set up a place for holistic beauty and nutritional advice here. *Rambla dels Ducs de Palma de Mallorca 7 | www.tolocrespi.es*

INSIDER TIP CHOCOLAT FACTORY (U D4) *(ω d4)*

This chocolate shop for sweet-toothed shoppers under sandstone vaults is super-trendy. *Plaça d'es Mercat 9 and Carrer Jaume II 1*

COLMADO SANTO DOMINGO (U C5) *(ω c5)*

Photogenic little shop in Palma's historic quarter selling *sobrasadas, jamón serrano* and other specialities. *Carrer Sant Domingo*

DESIGUAL (U D3) *(ω d3)*

Dark blue lighting brings out the bright youthful colours of the internationally famous Spanish Desigual brand. *Carrer San Miguel 12*

ESPECIAS CRESPI (U E4) *(ω e4)*

The oriental aromas emerging from Mallorca's most famous spice shop draw customers from far and wide. Over 150 different types of herbs and spices are sold by the packet, from basic oregano to expensive *azafrán* (saffron). *Via Sindicat 64*

SA FORMATGERIA (U C2) *(ω c2)*

This tiny shop creates a great stink, in the best possible way: just follow the aromas of countless Mediterranean cheeses wafting out the door. INSIDER TIP *Tabla mallorquina* with seven local cheeses to try! *Carrer Oms 30*

FORN DES TEATRE (U C4) *(ω c4)*

Palma's oldest bakery is resplendent in its opulent Art Nouveau decor, selling the best *ensaimadas* and *empanadas*. *Plaça Weyler 9*

ART GALLERIES

The art scene is vibrant and colourful. Here's a selection from over 30 relevant addresses in Palma: *Altair (Carrer Sant Jaume 23); Casal Solleric (Passeig des Born 27); Sa Nostra arts centre (Carrer Concepció 12); Sala Pelaires (Carrer Pelaires 23)*. The island's largest arts event takes place in September: the INSIDER TIP *Nit de l'Art*. A whole night is dedicated to the arts – in about 25 galleries, plus live music in the streets and a variety of culinary treats.

TABACOS ROIG (U B4) *(ω b4)*

Toni Roig's well-stocked tobacco shop is already a legend. Look no further for the world's most famous cigars, sold much cheaper than at home. *Passeig des Born 20*

For excellent pastries, look no further: the entrance to Palma's oldest bakery

MERCADILLO ECOLÓGICO ☺
(U D2) (𝄞 d2)

The island's first market selling exclusively organic produce is held on Saturdays on the *Plaça Obispo Berenguer de Palou*

ENTERTAINMENT

The cathedral, the castle and the harbour boulevard are lit up when the nightlife shifts up a gear after midnight in the *Sa Llotja* quarter, on the *Passeig Marítim* and in the *El Terreno* quarter. Whether your preference is just strolling around or being chauffeured from club to club by taxi – Palma's night scenery is bright and colourful.

ABACO (U B5) (𝄞 b5)

Many hold this to be Europe's most beautiful night club: the Abaco *(www. bar-abaco.com)* in the city palace.

There's no admission charge, but expect to pay through the nose for the fruit cocktails. *Carrer Sant Joan 1 | from 8pm onwards*

BARCELONA CAFÉ (U B5) (𝄞 b5)

This live jazz club might be tiny, it certainly is Palma's best. *Carrer Apuntadors 5 | from midnight onwards*

LA BODEGUITA DEL MEDIO
(U B5) (𝄞 F7)

Dance the night away in this wannabe Havana joint, whether salsa, Latino or... mojito. *Carrer Valseca 18 | from midnight onwards*

COCO LA NUIT (U D3) (𝄞 d3)

Fabulous transvestite show in extravagant ambience; the food doesn't quite convince. *Carrer Sant Miguel 79 | from 9pm | for tickets tel. 9 71 72 80 54*

MADE IN BRASIL (143 E4) (*Ⅲ E7*)
Hot, packed, in your face: how about a marathon of samba, rumba and pop music? *Passeig Marítim 21 | from 11pm onwards*

OPIO (143 E4) (*Ⅲ F7*)
Decked out all in white, this bar forms part of the Puro Design Hotel. Monday to Friday between 6 and 10pm, small

of town and port. *78 rooms | Avinguda Jaume III 9 | tel. 9 71 72 73 40 | www.hotel-almudaina.com | Moderate*

ARABELLA SHERATON GOLF HOTEL SON VIDA (143 E4) (*Ⅲ E7*)
Luxury hotel with its own excellent restaurant, the *Plat d'Or. 93 rooms and suites | 5 km outside the centre in the exclusive suburb of Son Vida | tel.*

Spend a relaxing evening in the bars and clubs of Palma

snacks are served with each drink. Wednesday to Saturday between 10pm and 2am a fine DJ gets those party feet moving. *Carrer Montenegro 2*

TITO'S ☼ (143 E4) (*Ⅲ E7*)
Legendary and pretty loud super-club boasting a glass elevator (and harbour views) | *Passeig Marítim | from midnight | admission 12–20 euros*

WHERE TO STAY

ALMUDAINA HOTEL (U B4) (*Ⅲ b4*)
Centrally located hotel, restored in 2009, with rooftop terrace and fabulous views

9 71 78 71 00 | www.starwoodhotels.com | Expensive

BORN (U C4) (*Ⅲ c4*)
This centrally located hotel operates from a restored 16th-century townhouse with a quiet patio. *29 rooms | Carrer Sant Jaume 3 | tel. 9 71 71 29 42 | Budget–Moderate*

CASTILLO HOTEL SON VIDA
(143 E4) (*Ⅲ E7*)
If this hotel was already the height of luxury, it is even more so now after its one-year restoration. Travellers not requiring one of the 182 luxury suites or rooms nor

their own butler should still take advantage of the ● **INSIDER TIP** unique beautiful views of Palma from the ☼ terrace of this exclusive establishment. Your coffee will be served to right royal standards. *Son Vida | tel. 9 71 60 60 29 | www.hotel-sonvida.com | Expensive*

CORONA (143 E4) *(Ø E7)*

Long-established guesthouse with garden in the slightly down-at-heel El Terreno quarter, particularly suited to younger people; quiet location. *10 rooms, Art Deco suite with sea views | Carrer Josep Villalonga 22 | tel. 9 71 73 19 35 | Budget*

INSIDER TIP HOSTAL REGINA
(U D2) *(Ø d2)*

Basic but clean guesthouse with heating near Plaça Espanya. Ten rooms and genial British owners. No breakfast. *Carrer de Sant Miquel 77 | tel. 9 71 71 37 03 | www.hostalreginapalma.com | Budget*

HOSTAL RITZI (U B5) *(Ø b5)*

Located in the Apuntadores entertainment and food mile, this basic accommodation makes up for the lack of breakfast with a pretty patio. *17 rooms | Carrer Apuntadors 6 | tel. 9 71 71 46 10 | www.hostalritzi.com | Budget*

FOMENTO DE TURISMO
(U C5) *(Ø c5)*
Carrer Constitució 1 | tel. 9 71 72 53 96 | www.fomentmallorca.org

WHERE TO GO

BANYALBUFAR/ESTELLENCS ★
(143 D2) *(Ø D5–6)*

These two rock-solid villages of Arabic origin still cling to the mountain high above the sea. Situated on the bendy Ma-10 coastal road along romantic terraces dating back to Moorish times, they are best explored on foot, up some steps, down some more steps. Situated some 25 km northwest of Palma, Banyalbufar (pop. 630) offers local dishes from the well-run if overpriced *Son Tomas* restaurant *(closed Tue | Budget)*. Find fairer prices, as well as a pretty panoramic terrace and tasty cakes, at the Bellavista at the entrance to the village. An idyllic place to stay in the village of Estellencs is the Hotel *Nord (8 rooms | tel. 9 71 14 90 06 | www.hotelruralnord.com | Moderate)*. Both villages boast romantic if difficult-to-access tiny coves with waterfalls (signposted).

GUIDED TOURS

They are fire-engine red open-topped double deckers, the buses of the line 50 connecting all the capital's most important sights, from the cathedral to the Castell de Bellver. The complete route takes 80 minutes. Your 24-hour ticket allows you to hop on and off as you like at 16 stops. Earphones provide a recorded commentary in good English. *Every 20 minutes between 9.30am and*

10pm (Nov–March 10am–1pm), 20 euros per person.
'Strolls through History' is the name given to the two-hour city walks with a well-informed guide (costing 10 euros). The Jewish quarter, the monasteries, the port quarter, Art Nouveau and monumental buildings are the themes covered. Information (also for English-speakers) *tel. 9 71 72 07 20*

BUNYOLA/ALFABIA/RAIXA

(138 C5–6) (*ⳢⳢ F5*)

Occupying an idyllic position on the southern foothills of the Serra d'Alfabia, the village of Bunyola (pop. 6000), 35 km north of Palma, has its own nostalgic station on the Sóller railway. The Catalan *Ses Porxeres* restaurant you see before you enter the motorway tunnel to Sóller *(tel. 971613762 | closed Sun, Mon and Aug | Moderate–Expensive)* is famous for starters that cover the entire table and good Catalan cuisine. Next door, the *Jardins d'Alfabia* containing a 17th-century country house are

Terraced gardens on the wild steep coast of Banyalbufar

Mallorca's best-preserved testimony to the skill of Arab garden designers *(on the Ma11 at km 17 | Mon–Fri 9.30am–5.30pm, Sat 9.30am–1pm | admission 4.50 euros | www.jardinesdealfabia.com)*. The ● historic *Raixa* family estate is today in government hands and being restored piece by piece. Evil Under the Sun, a movie based on an Agatha Christie thriller, was filmed here. When the fashion designer Jil Sander tried to purchase it, for a tidy sum, the Balearic government intervened to keep it from falling into foreign hands, buying it from the last private owners. *At km 12 on the Ma11 | visits by previous appointment Mon–Fri 10am–2pm, Sat/Sun 10am–2pm admission free with guided tour; no previous appointment necessary | tel. 971947320 | www.raixa.cat*

CIUTAT JARDÍ (143 F4) (*ⳢⳢ F8*)

On weekends in particular, the locals descend on this villa suburb east of Palma, and it's easy to see why: a location right by the sea with a pretty swimming beach and the 'foodie mile' behind it, with excellent fish restaurants, such as *Casa Fernando (tel. 971265417 | closed Mon | Expensive)*, serving grilled fish and seafood straight off the boat that restaurant guests may INSIDER TIP pick themselves at the counter. The place brings together tourists and business people. On the beach, with fabulous views of Palma Bay and food straight out of the sea, look out for the *Restaurante Bungalow (tel. 971262738 | closed Mon | Moderate)*.

ESPORLES/SA GRANJA

(143 D–E2) (*ⳢⳢ E5–6*)

The long-drawn-out village of Esporles (pop. 4800) lies in a fertile, evergreen valley some 15 km northwest of Palma. The former post office was turned first into a hostal and in 2005 into a design hotel by the name of *L'Estada (on the church square | tel. 9 71 61 02 02 | www. hotelestada.com | Moderate)* with seven pretty rooms and two suites. The in-house garden restaurant serves fine re-gional cuisine using fresh island produce. Situated around 1.5 km north of Espor-les, the country estate of *Sa Granja (daily 10am–7pm, in winter to 6pm | admission 11 euros, Wed and Fri 13 euros | www. lagranja.net)* dates back to Roman and Arab times. Since the 1970s the place has been an open-air museum showing workshops as well as the salons of the nobility. On Wednesdays and Fridays the craftsmen slip on traditional garb to do their work.

FESTIVAL PARC (144 A4) (*m G6*)
The fancy name hides a shopping centre with over 30 outlet stores of well-known brands as well as an entertainment centre with crazy golf, bowling, gam-bling halls, restaurants and 20 cinema screens. *Motorway exit Marratxí/sa Cabaneta, right at the exit on the left-hand side of the motorway (coming from Palma)*

GENOVA (143 E4) (*m E7*)
With its many authentic cosy bars and restaurants, this western suburb of Pal-ma is foodie heaven. Genova also boasts a romantic location amongst flights of steps and terraces. The largest eatery, consisting of two places, is *Mesón Can Pedro (tel. 9 71 40 24 79 | closed Thu | Budget)* with a charcoal barbecue.

PLATJA DE PALMA/S'ARENAL
(144 A6) (*m G8*)
This is a famous, even infamous place for watching German tourists making fools of themselves: the *balneario (beach sec-tion) 6,* or 'Ballermann' where in sum-

Sa Granja shows the way it used to be

mer in particular the sounds of beery German joviality fill the air. Right behind it, pub after bar after pub line the *Bier-strasse and Schinkenstrasse ('Beer' and 'Ham Roads'),* controlled with an iron fist by the local *Bierkönig* ('King of Beer'). After moving into Ham Road from Lluc-major, the Bavarian deli eatery *s'Olivera den Louis (tel. 6 51 72 38 07 | www.louiso livera.de | open every day | Budget–Mod-erate)* still offers a good-value Bavarian **INSIDER TIP** Sunday brunch in summer. The sweeping 8 km sandy beach, divided into 16 *balnearios* in total, and its palm-lined promenade loses appeal slightly due to near-seamless hotels offering 43,000 beds in total. Nearly all are in the hands of tour operators, first and foremost the eight well-run establishments of the RIU chain. Nowhere on the island is the tourist infrastructure as perfect as on *Platja de Palma*. However, Palma's city government is keen to deal with its many superannuated hotel buildings. In 2010, a plan to upgrade the Platja was published, looking to pull down many private houses and to halve the number of hotel beds. Protests on the part of those affected have led to the project being put on ice for the time being.

The *Megapark* is a gigantic party mecca in a neo-Gothic edifice that can fit in up to 8000 guests – now, however, the nighttime musical entertainment is all happening underground. In *Arenal,* right at the end of the bay, young people can find good-value accommodation in simple guesthouses. A simple but clean choice is the *Alberg Platja de Palma (Carrer Costa Brava 13 | tel. 9 71 26 08 92 | Budget)*. A worthwhile change from the mostly German or international fare is on offer at *Rancho Picadero, Can Pastilla (Carrer Flamenco 1 | tel. 9 71 26 10 02 | open every day | Moderate)*.

PORT DE PORTALS ★ (143 E5) (*Ø E8*)
The exclusive marina below Portals Nous acts like a magnet for all who want to see and be seen, including Spain's royal family; mooring fees are the most expensive on the island. Add to the mix the harbour boulevard with its high-end boutiques and expensive restaurants, such as *Tristan (tel. 9 71 67 55 47 | www. tristan-restaurant.com | in winter closed Mon, also early–mid Dec | Expensive)*. Famous for Gerhard Schwaiger's excellent Mediterranean cuisine, it has prices to match, and reservation is required. *Diablito (tel. 9 71 67 94 00 | open every day | Moderate)* is mainly frequented by young people ordering huge pizzas. *Wellie's (tel. 9 71 67 64 44 | open every day | Moderate)* is the (overpriced) meeting place for an evening *copa*, and serves copious salad platters. For excellent Mediterranean food head for the bistro at *Flanigan's (open every day)*, but it might be a good idea to check out the prices on the menu! 2200 euros (butler included) is the rate charged for the presidential suite in the *Sant Regis Mardavall Hotel (133 rooms | tel. 9 71 62 96 29 | www.mardavall-hotel. com | Expensive)*. Outside high season music-loving gourmets will enjoy the

BOOKS & FILMS

▶ **A Winter in Mallorca** – describes the love-hate relationship that George Sand had with the island and its inhabitants in the winter of 1838–39, which she experienced – and suffered – with her lover Frédéric Chopin in Palma and Valldemossa: a must-read.

▶ **The Bloody Bockara** – is the name of the first detective novel by American hotelier George Scott. It's an exciting read,

and the original idea of selling the book together with a good bottle of Binissalem *vino tinto* turns it into a Mallorca thriller pack with benefits.

▶ **Snowball Oranges** – Peter Kerr describes what it was like to exchange the Scottish climate for a winter in Mallorca. This humorous account of life on the island was the first of five in a bestselling series.

INSIDER TIP Sunday jazz brunch *(1–4pm)* for only 35 euros at the buffet of the *Lindner Golf und Wellness Resort Hotel (tel. 9 71 70 77 77 | www.lindner.de/en/ | Expensive)*.

PÓRTOL/SA CABANETA

(144 A–B4) *(ᨑ G6–7)*

This twin village 6 km south of Santa Maria (pop. 8000) is famous for its pottery and ceramics workshops. The way to the eight *olleríes* in Pórtol, producing bellied *olles* and flat *greixoneras* is signposted. INSIDER TIP *L'Albello* at the edge of the village has the largest selection. The workshops of *sa Cabaneta,* hidden in the upper part of the village, are famous for their *siurell figurines.*

SANTA EUGÈNIA (144 C4) *(ᨑ H6)*

A drive here is recommended not for the sake of the village, which is nothing special, but for a visit to the ☺ *Natura Parc* with its large enclosures. The owners campaign for conservation of threatened animal species and ecological awareness, also offering specific education programmes for schoolchildren. The biggest attraction of the small zoo is a butterfly house. *At km 15.4 on the country road to Sineu, 7.5 km southeast of Santa Maria | daily 10am–6pm | admission 9 euros*

SANTA MARIA DEL CAMÍ

(144 B3–4) *(ᨑ H6)*

15 km northeast of Palma, this town of 5100 inhabitants is surrounded by the fincas of international residents. It is worth taking a look at the small 17th-century cloisters, the large Sunday market and visiting one of the tapas tavernas on the Ma13A thoroughfare. *Sa Font* is the tapas bar with the longest counter and the biggest choice, *Budget*. The INSIDER TIP originally painted inte-

Classy mooring for classy yachts: Port de Portals

rior of the *Bacchus* restaurant with its creative Mediterranean cuisine alone would make a visit to *Read's Hotel & Spa (Carretera Santa Maria–Alaró s/n | tel. 9 71 14 02 61 | www.readshotel.com | Expensive)*, worthwhile. Established 500 years ago, this luxury country hotel has 23 rooms and boasts a magnificent English garden.

There are only two linen weavers left on the island. *Artesania textil Bujosa (Carrer Bernardo Santa Eugènia 53)* is the only one to still manufacture traditional *ikats* by hand; this is of course reflected in the price.

ANDRATX

(142 B4) *(ⅆ C7)* **In the shade of a sturdy fortified church, framed by pine-covered hills, the country town of Andratx (pop. 7000) remains in a gentle snooze most of the time.**

Apart from Wednesdays, when there's a market on, you won't meet many tourists here; they prefer *Port d'Andratx* (pop. 3000), 5 km away. It is extremely built-up, and in 2006 corruption scandals related to this made headlines; the matter is still with the courts.

SIGHTSEEING

CALA LLAMP/SA MOLA

Check out the level of (nouveau) richness in such a small area even if you only do it once! The hilly back country between the Sa Mola peninsula and the steep coast above the cliff-fringed bay of Cala Llamp is an oversized construction site of breathtaking luxury villas.

CENTRE CULTURAL

Works by contemporary artists are on show in the large, light-filled spaces of a restored finca. *Carretera Andratx–Capdella at km 1.5 | Tue–Sat 10am–6pm, Sun 10am–4pm*

STUDIO WEIL

At the end of the port road to La Mola, this white asymmetric building comes as an architectural surprise. It is a INSIDER**TIP** studio with gallery built by star architect Daniel Libeskind for artist Barbara Weil. *Camí de Sant Carles 20 | Sat/Sun 11.30am–2pm and 4–6pm | www.studioweil.com*

FOOD & DRINK

LAYN

This eatery in an old villa with courtyard and terrace right on the harbour has been in the hands of the same family for generations, and been renovated many times; it remains a reliable choice. Enjoy tasty regional cuisine served by attentive staff. *Harbour boulevard | tel. 9 71 67 18 55 | www.layn.net | open every day | Moderate*

MARISQUERÍA GALICIA

This cosy and popular taverna serves tasty grilled fish; an excellent choice, for instance, is Galician-style squid fried in garlic oil. One word of warning: make sure you don't confuse it with the more expensive place of the same name – in

the same street! *Carrer Isaac Peral 37 | tel. 9 71 67 27 05 | open every day | Budget–Moderate*

EL PATIO

Renovated in 2010 after five years of standing empty, a restaurant once famous across the island is trying to win fame again. The strategy revolves around fine Mediterranean cuisine based on fresh island produce. *Carretera Andratx–Port d'Andratx (Ma1), km 30.5 | tel. 9 71 67 17 03 |www.restaurante-elpatio.com | closed Tue/Wed | Expensive*

WHERE TO STAY

CATALINA VERA

Simple, but pretty clean hostal with garden in the port area; all rooms have a balcony or terrace. *20 rooms | Carrer Isaac Peral 63 | tel. 9 71 67 19 18 | www.hostalcatalinavera.es | closed Nov–March | Budget*

MON PORT HOTEL

Comfortable hotel with spa on the edge of Port d'Andratx. *139 rooms and suites | Cala d'Egos | tel. 9 71 23 86 23 | www.hotelmonport.com | Moderate–Expensive*

VILLA ITALIA

Befitting the refined ambience, this 1920s villa lording it over the port was converted into a stylish exclusive hotel with a later 'Castillo' extension, spa, restaurant and cocktail bar. *22 apartments and suites | Camino de San Carlos 13 | tel. 9 71 67 40 11 | www.hotelvillaitalia.com | Expensive*

Port d'Andratx attracts 'sea and be seen' folk alike

Sa Dragonera: what would hiking be without those breaks in between?

WHERE TO GO

CAMP DE MAR (142 B5) (⋔ C6)

A wooded bendy road with pretty views connects Port d'Andratx with Camp de Mar (pop. 250) 4.5 km away, which over the past few years has seen much development and become quite refined. The comfortable *RIU Camp de Mar* hotel (293 rooms | tel. 9 71 23 52 00 | *Moderate*), one of the most beautiful houses in this chain, lies right on the beach of light-coloured sand.

The *Royal Golfresort & Spa Dorint Sofitel* with 162 bright, pleasant and luxurious rooms and two suites (tel. 9 71 13 65 65 | *www. dorintresorts.com/camp-de-mar-mal lorca | Expensive)* has been integrated into the *Golf de Andratx* 18-hole links (charging a steep 100 euros for the green fee). Light Mediterranean dishes can be had at the bistro forming part of

Jens *(Camp de Capllonch Plome 10 | tel. 9 71 23 63 06 | Moderate)*.

SANT ELM/SA DRAGONERA ☺
(142 A4) (⋔ A–B7)

The best thing about the small seaside resort of Sant Elm (pop. 250) 8 km west of Andratx is its tranquillity – and the view of the offshore island of ★ *Sa Dragonera*. In summer, Sa Dragonera can be reached by the ferry Margarita in about 20 minutes *(Tue–Sun, from 10.15am five times a day, last return by arrangement | tel. 6 96 42 39 33 | 9 euros)*. The strictly protected islet, 4.2 km long, up to 1 km wide with natural history museum and hiking trails, is home to endemic lizards and many types of bird. From Sant Elm not one but three hiking trails lead to the monastery of *Sa Trapa* (with refuge and managed by the GOB). The *Vistamar* restaurant with terrace above the mini harbour *(tel. 9 71 23 75 47 | closed on Tue | Moderate)* serves fabulous **INSIDER TIP** *Paella de Mariscos*.

PALMA NOVA/ MAGALUF

(143 D5) (*M D8*) This huge resort belongs to Calvià, whose 51,000 inhabitants form part of the island's second-largest municipality, and one of the wealthiest in Europe.

The wealth stems from tourism and tax revenues of rich finca owners. Just under 30,000 of Calvià's 60,000 hotel beds are concentrated here, making the stacked hotels, pubs and snack bars fairly faceless. The beaches however are long, wide and pretty. This is British partyville, with action and showparks providing entertainment.

FOOD & DRINK

CIRO'S
Long-established if modernised large restaurant, with a terrace and sea views and good Mediterranean cuisine. *Paseo del Mar 3 | tel. 9 71 68 10 52 | open every day | Moderate*

LEISURE & SPORTS

GOLF DE PONIENTE
This 18-hole course on the edge of Magaluf requires some expertise; green fee 88 euros. *tel. 9 71 13 01 48 | www.ponientegolf.com*

WESTERN WATER PARK
Trumping the neighbouring Aquaparc, this lively water park has a Western show and breathtaking tower dives. *On the edge of Magaluf | daily 10am–5pm, in midsummer to 6pm | admission 25 euros | www.westernpark.com*

ENTERTAINMENT

The nightlife here is somewhat in line with the cut-price hotels. Youngsters go for the *BCM* superclub *(daily 10pm–5am)*. The former *Casino de Mallorca* in the well-heeled neighbouring town of Portals Vells, 7 km to the south, has moved to Palma, into the Porto Pi part of town, into the shopping centre of the same name.

WHERE TO STAY

INSIDER TIP ▶ SON CALIU HOTEL SPA-OASIS
It's all in the name: this spa and wellness centre is fabulous! 20 euros gets even non-residents a whole day of pampering. There are 221 rooms and suites, while top service makes up for the small size of the beach. *Avinguda Son Caliu 8 | tel. 9 71 68 22 00 | www.soncaliu.com | Moderate–Expensive*

WHERE TO GO

SANTA PONÇA (142 C5) (*M D8*)
This resort too has nearly fused with Magaluf, another tourist ghetto for British and German guests. The triple-A course *Golf Santa Ponça 1, 2 and 3* sees a fair number of VIPs. The only public golf course *(no. 3 with 9 holes, green fee 40 euros)* frames the golfers' hotel *Golf Santa Ponça (18 rooms | tel. 9 71 69 02 11 | Expensive)*.

PEGUERA

(142 C5) (*M C8*) Peguera (pop. 3500) has always been a magnet for German tourists; maybe because the resort boasts pretty hiking trails and dreamy mountain villages in its hilly back country.

The town has also gained from seeing

its former thoroughfare turned into a pedestrianised promenade. Along the *Bulevar* you will find bars and restaurants, boutiques and souvenir shops. At the end of the last century, Peguera was a bastion of so-called hibernators or long-term vacationers. Today, visitors are that bit younger, and the town is now also attracting visitors on activity holidays who flock to the island's largest tennis centre or on one of the five golf courses in the vicinity. Considering the number of visitors Peguera receives, the beaches are fairly small.

FOOD & DRINK

BIERGARTEN ES FASSET
Diners come not only for the pizzas, but also for the tasty tapas and Spanish live music. *Carrer Eucaliptus 5 | tel. 971 68 71 71 | open every day | Budget*

ENTERTAINMENT

DISCOTECA RENDEZVOUS
Meeting point for more mature clubbers *(www.discorendezvous.com)* on Peguera's main promenade. *Daily, 10pm–6am*

WHERE TO STAY

ALDEA 2 CALA FORNELLS
Designed by star architect Pedro Otzup, this slightly labyrinthine complex is lo-

RAMÓN LLULL

You'll be hard pressed to find a village on the island without a street named after Ramón Llull. Born around 1232 in Palma as the son of a Mallorcan nobleman, he was converted aged 30 by a vision, living forthwith as a Franciscan monk and scholar. Llull worked as a missionary in North Africa and Asia Minor, and founded a school for priests and missionaries near Valldemossa, as well as a school for Oriental languages. Llull's ideal of understanding between people of different creeds, whether Christians, Muslims, Jews or pagans, encountered strong resistance. The Mallorcans revere Llull however more as the author of prose in the Catalan language, which he elevated to the status of a literary language through works such as the philosophical novel Blanquerna.

Popular with tourists, but very busy in high season: Peguera

cated about 1.5 km west of Peguera high above the sea. The apartments have different views and quality ranging from excellent to middling. *85 apartments | tel. 9 71 68 69 50 | Moderate*

VILLA ANA

One example of the many simple family guesthouses in Peguera. Clean. *35 rooms | Carrer Gaviotas 13 | tel. 9 71 68 67 49 | Budget*

VILLAMIL

Part of the Hesperia chain, this comfortable beach hotel has been restored several times and boasts a pretty suite with sea view on the top floor. *125 rooms | tel. 9 71 68 60 50 | www.hesperia.com Expensive*

WHERE TO GO

GALILEA/PUIGPUNYENT ☀
(143 D3) (*Ø D6–7*)

Galilea's biblical name stands for a blissful retreat. The airy terraced village (pop. 300) some 15 km northeast of Peguera serves as an idyllic second home to many foreigners whose houses offer fine views towards the sea. Guests of the small charming hotel *Scott's Galilea (Sa Mola Gran, s/n | tel. 9 71 61 41 70 | www.scottsgalilea.com | Expensive)* with ten comfy studios and apartments, plus swimming pool, are treated to equally lovely views.

4 km across a small pass divide Galilea and *Puigpunyent* (pop. 1400). One of the fine old estates dotted around the village has been converted by its American owner into a fairly ostentatious ho-

tel. The *Gran Hotel Son Net* represents the height of luxury with six suites (the most expensive costing 1240 euros), 18 double rooms and a few holiday cottages; a gourmet restaurant complements the ensemble *(tel. 9 71 14 70 00 | www.sonnet.es | Expensive)*.

VALLDEMOSSA

(143 E1) (*ω E–F5*) Travelling from Palma on the recently widened Ma1110, the view of the ● mountain village of Valldemossa (pop. 2000) will take your breath away again and again.

The summer palace King Jaume II had built here was extended by his son and successor Sancho I. Today still, the narrow houses on stone terraces with flowering gardens, crowned by the parish church and the famous charterhouse continue to fascinate visitors. If you haven't seen this village you haven't seen Mallorca.

SIGHTSEEING

COSTA NORD DE VALLDEMOSSA

This arts centre founded by Michael Douglas provides an American perspective on the life of Archduke Ludwig Salvator and the wild northwest of Mallorca; the centre also hosts big musical events. *At the village entrance coming from Palma | daily 9.30am–6pm | admission 5 euros*

FUNDACIÓ CULTURAL COLL BARDOLET

The most enchanting feature here are the INSIDER TIP paintings showing dance scenes by Coll Bardolet, the Catalan painter who lived in Valldemossa up to his death in 2007. In accordance with his wishes part of his work was transferred to the art foundation that bears his name. It has found a worthy home at Carrer Bl-

anquerna 4 (main street). *Mon–Sat Nov–March 10am–4pm, April–Oct 10am–2pm and 3–7pm, Sun 10am–4pm or 8pm | free of charge | www.fccollbardolet.org*

REAL CARTUJA

Every year, over 300,000 tourists shuffle through the charterhouse monastery on the trail of Frédéric Chopin and George Sand who spent six cold and wet weeks here in winter 1838–39. INSIDER TIP Before half past ten and from four o'clock onwards you can admire notes, books, paintings, piano and bust in peace and quiet. From 1399 up to its secularisation in 1835, the former royal residence was a charterhouse. The building we see today dates from the 18th century. The old monastic pharmacy is well worth seeing. Don't miss the *Palau de Rei Sanxo* either, for its precious furnishings and maybe a short piano concert. *Mon–Sat 9.30am–6.30pm (in winter 4.30pm), Sun 10am–1pm; the circuit of a good 1.5 hours costs 8.50 euros.*

LOWER VILLAGE

No other island village is adorned with as many flowers as ★ *Valldemossa's lower village* with its Gothic parish church of Sant Bartomeu. The decorative tiles on every house depict scenes from the life of Santa Catalina, born in Carrer Rectoría and canonised in 1930. The former maidservant Catalina Tomàs (1531–74) has been honoured with a charming monument next to the parish church. Mallorcans drive for miles to see her – and buy some *cocas de patata*, potato doughnuts available in any bakery.

FOOD & DRINK
WHERE TO STAY

CAN MARIO

Established in 1890, the oldest hostelry in town is simple and easy-going.

8 rooms | Carrer Uetam 8 | tel. 9 71 61 21 22 | www.hostalcanmario.net | Budget

VALLDEMOSSA ☆

Blessed with a spectacular location on the slope of a hill and an excellent restaurant (go for the set menu!), three rooms and seven suites, this finca hotel is a place fit for a king, including views of the Real Cartuja and the surrounding mountains. *Carretera Vieja de Valldemossa s/n | tel. 9 71 61 26 26 | www. valldemossahotelrural.com | Expensive*

WHERE TO GO

ELS ERMITANS ☆ (143 E1) (*∅ E5*)

Founded in 1648, the tiny hermitage offers terrific views of sea and coast. Today still, hermits live here, following the rules of saints Paul and Anthony. The car is best left at the car park below; the romantic if narrow and bendy road can be tackled on foot (around 20 mins). *Around 3 km north on the Deià road, a narrow drive opposite the Can Costa restaurant*

PORT DE VALLDEMOSSA
(143 E1) (*∅ E5*)

Tiny and romantic, this pebbly harbour bay, suitable for swimming, is reached after 7 km of driving on hairpin bends (signposted turn-off from the Ma10. Visitors travelling in a large hire car and feeling a bit nervous should avoid this – the only – access road!) Try the *Es Port beach tavern*, ask for fresh fish and order a side dish of *frito* in a clay pot: *muy bien! Opening times vary | tel. 9 71 61 61 94 | Moderate*

Attracts hundreds of thousands of visitors every year: the charterhouse monastery in Valldemossa

TRIPS & TOURS

The tours are marked in green in the road atlas, pull-out map and on the back cover

1 ON THE SMUGGLERS' TRAIL

This easy hike follows an old smugglers' path from Bany-albufar to the harbour of Port des Canonge and back. This tour takes about three hours without breaks.

Mallorca is a hikers' paradise. Whilst land is more or less in private hands, a special right of way bars landowners from making their forests and mountains inaccessible. This has meant the opening up of former shepherds' and pilgrims' tracks, hunters' trails and smugglers' paths. The mixture of mountain and sea is captivating, as is the vegetation. Of the dozens of charming hiking trails to choose from, ranging from an easy stroll along

the coast to adventurous hikes through deeply cut gorges, this is an example of a simple, but very varied hike.

The starting point is a small car park in an S-bend between kilometre 85 and 86 on the Ma10 high above the mountain village of Banyalbufar → p. 93, whose terraces of Moorish origin, planted with vegetables and Malvasia vines, you will see from above after a few metres.

The entire path is signposted with an arrow on wooden posts. A shady forest of Aleppo pines means that even in summer this tour is not too demanding. The broad path is covered with pine needles, which make it pleasantly soft and put a spring in your step. In Franco's time this path was used by smugglers to transport cigarettes, alcohol and coffee by

Experience nature and culture to the full: follow dream routes by car, and historic byways on foot

the sackful from the sea into their hideaways; let your imagination run free!

Down below, the blue sea twinkles again and again between the green treetops. Depending on the time of year, you will see purple heather flowering on the wayside, the flame-red fruit of arbutus 'strawberry' trees ripening, or green *ginebrós,* juniper berries from which a delicious gin is distilled.

Where the path leads through the holm oaks, long-extinct professions come to life again: a *sitga,* the circular area where charcoal was burnt, had a rush-covered shelter for the lime burners who had to be present day and night. Look out for the ruin of a forn de calç lime kiln, where in the olden days the lime burners made lime for whitening their houses from the limestone rock. Imperceptibly, the path gently leads downhill for half an hour to reach a huge rock wall, where stalactites and stalagmites can be seen in the limestone. On days when the sea is restless, the wall amplifies the thunderous sound of the waves.

A little later rocky crags – bizarre, wild, and romantic – appear far below above the sea, with wind-bent pines clinging on. White spray breaks onto the rocky shore, while now and again a boat crosses the wide blue sea. And far in the distance you can spot the small peninsula of na Foradada, where once upon a time Archduke Ludwig Salvator set foot on Mallorca and started discovering the place for himself.

From this point onwards it's downhill all the way, past the huge 400-year old **Son Bunyola**. This country estate was purchased by a British billionaire in order build a luxury finca hotel here – he's still waiting for planning permission... And then finally you reach the sea, crystal clear, with a pebble beach and tons of flotsam and jetsam. Jump in, with or without swimming togs. A dream! Or maybe wait till you're on the way back; there is still a part of the trail to go, passing some myrtle bushes, before you reach tiny **Port des Canonge**.

At the height of summer it is more animated, at weekends in particular when Mallorcan daytrippers often find their way here. The rest of the time it is very quiet here – which is part of its considerable charm. The port is lined by red rocks licked into a round shape by the sea and seaweed; the smell of fish and salt hangs in the air. There might be a fisherman dozing in the shade of a boat tarpaulin: this is a peaceful place at the end of the world.

Hungry hikers, maybe carrying no provisions, should walk up the main street, past the *Toni* restaurant, and take a break in **Cana Madó**. While none too pretty, this eatery is completely down-to-earth. Order a few tapas and a glass of the excellent white wine, watch the cats weaving in and out of your legs, and banish from your mind for a moment the fact that after refreshments you'll have to trek back the entire way you came, and uphill at that.

Rest assured that the way back opens up entirely new vistas, with entirely different things waiting to be spotted along the wayside. And don't forget to visit **Banyalbufar → p. 93** after your return, even if it's only a stop at the Bellavista café's rooftop terrace – as an unhurried finish to an eventful day.

2 THE COUNTRY AND ITS PEOPLE: FARMERS, WINEMAKERS, FISHERMEN

 This 125-km day trip by car leads right into the island's interior. Feel free to spread the journey over several days. From Sineu, we travel across the great plain of Es Plá and then deep into the south: you'll meet islanders who are hardly involved in tourism, if at all. That doesn't mean there are no beaches; don't forget to pack your swimming togs.

The starting point is **Sineu → p. 80** in the geographical centre of the island. The best day for this trip is a Wednesday, as farmers from far and wide flock to the island's oldest and most important cattle market. If you get there really early, around 8.30am, you can witness the haggling for chicks and cows, sheep and pigs. Come 10am, when entire coachloads of tourists pour into the market you should already be 7 km further south, in **Sant Joan**. In the centre of the village follow the sign saying *Els Calderés* which leads to a splendid estate, converted into a finca museum in 1992.

A huge wine cellar (offering tastings too) is testimony to the times when winemaking was profitable here; the industry was destroyed when the phylloxera pest hit at the beginning of the 20th century, but there have been attempts to start up again. The switch from wine to wheat in the last century is illustrated by an enor-

Ma15 vineyards take their place. The area around Petra, Porreres and Felanitx is a centre for producing white wines. After

Sunday shopping: market day in the historic centre of Felanitx

mous granary on the first floor which also shows the other agricultural products of the estate. The entrance charge is well worth paying, especially as the interesting interior, several hundred years old, has remained completely intact.

Further on, going south, the drive takes you through the municipality of **Vilafranca** where smoke-blackened kilns and piles of *tejas* (slates) tell of an old and still practised trade, brick manufacturing. While the road up to now led past broad wheat fields, almond, fig and carob tree plantations, once you've crossed the

about 11 km you will see the country town of **Felanitx** → p. 55 with its characteristic mill stumps. The port of Felanitx, **Portocolom** → p. 58, lies 13 km southeast. Its funnel-shaped harbour is framed by the **INSIDER TIP** colourfully painted boat sheds of the fishermen. A place that serves fresh fish straight off the boat is the **Sa Sinia** restaurant *(tel. 971 82 43 23 | closed Mon | Expensive)* right on the harbour. Carry on through the Serra de Llevant, the flower-bedecked villages of S'Horta, Calonge and S'Alquería Blanca. From Calonge, you can take a detour to the **Cala d'Or** → p. 70 resort with its several small beaches. In the port of Cala d'Or, the best fish and a wonderful tasting menu for 65 euros at the excellent *Port Petit (tel. 9 71 64 30 39 | www. portpetit.com | March/April closed Tue | Expensive)* is fit for a king: the Spanish king has already graced this place with his presence. The nicely laid-out TUI-Robinson Club 😊 Cala Serena § *(280 rooms)* near Cala d'Or *(Moderate–Expensive | www.robinson.com)* is an environmental pioneer, boasting solar power, recycling and reduced use of drinking water.

Drive back to Calonge and on to S'Alquería Blanca to the entrance to the village of **Santanyí** → p. 69. Here you follow the sign pointing towards Cala S'Amarador/Cala Mondragó. After 5 km,

this road, so typical for the south of the island and fringed by quarry-stone walls *(parets seques)*, ends at the barrier of the car park of **Cala Mondragó** → p. 71. Another 500 m on foot through aromatic pine forest takes you to the two magnificent swimming bays at the back, which unfortunately tend to get very busy in summer. The **Parc Natural Mondrago** → p. 71 *(daily 9am–4pm)* shelters some 70 types of birds, as well as plants and animals threatened by extinction, such as a number of tortoise species and the genet, cat-like animals related to civets. The park can also be explored on foot or by bike.

On the way back to Santanyí, a road turns off left to the small holiday village of **Cala Figuera** → p. 70, the next

This tour features inviting coves with fine sandy beaches

destination and the second port on this tour. In the afternoon you may watch the fishing boats return with their catch. The *Bon Bar* offers not only lovely views of the port, but also fine ice cream. Occupying an exposed position high above the sea, the *Rocamar* hotel *(42 rooms | tel. | 9 71 64 51 25 | www.rocamarplayamar. com | Budget)* has a swimming pool and private access to the water.

Next door, high above the entrance to the port, the *Villa Sierena Hotel* has 45 rooms and 19 apartments, a pool, restaurant and private beach access *(tel. 9 71 64 53 03 | www.hotelvillasirena.com | Moderate)*.

Back in Santanyí follow the signpost to the Colònia de Sant Jordi to reach, via the hamlet of Llombards, the village of **Ses Salines** → p. 71. To visit the southern tip of the island first and take a longer walk, turn left shortly after Llombards onto the Ma-6110. Ten kilometres on you will reach the *Cap de Ses Salines.* The drive is worth doing, not so much for the lighthouse, but for a fine path leading along the sea to completely pristine beaches. After about half an hour's hike you will be rewarded by the sight of the snow-white **INSIDERTIP** Platja des Caragol (bring sun protection!), followed, after another half hour, by the lonely *Cala Entugores*, fringed by marram grass. Both beaches are frequented by nudists. It is a drive of about 12 km from Cap de Ses Salines to the village of Ses Salines. If the weather isn't great for swimming on the day of your drive, you could visit either **Botanicactus** → p. 72 with its hundreds of types of cacti or pop into *Manolo's* chaotic gourmet universe: **Casa Manolo** | *tel. 9 71 64 91 30 | closed Mon | Moderate–Expensive*. Always full, always crammed, but always excellent, this tiny tavern specialises in grilled seafood and delicacies prepared in the earthenware

greixonera. The **INSIDERTIP** arròs de notario takes its name from the village solicitor who is said to have always insisted on seeing his rice dish given a touch of refinement with lobster. We are indebted

It's not only cacti that grow at Botanicactus

to him and Manolo – connoisseurs drive for miles for this.

If you'd still like to continue, drive on towards Campos. After 4 km you reach a crossroads; here, turn left following the sign for *Colònia de Sant Jordi* and fork off right after about 1 km towards **Es Trenc** → p. 67. Here, the island is completely flat and nearly treeless. You are now entering the quietness of the saline lakes, the **Salines de Llevant** → p. 73, where the silence is only broken by the cries of birds. White piles of salt and the pink-blue evaporation lakes shelter the sandy beach of Es Trenc, where not a single building spoils the scenery. Another beach saved thanks to a GOB initiative, this is a good place to finish the day, in dunes and the turquoise-coloured water of a beautiful crescent-shaped bay, which towards evening, when there are fewer visitors, is truly scenery from a dream.

The return route leads you via **Campos** → p. 64 and Felanitx back to Sineu.

SPORTS & ACTIVITIES

Once the thermometer hits the 40-degree mark, many holidaymakers feel the only way to go is down to the sea.
No wonder watersports such as swimming, diving, sailing and windsurfing top visitors' wish lists, at least in the summer months. Many tourism managers have mixed feelings about this: they want Mallorca to be an all-year-round destination. The buzzword now is 'activity holiday'. Given that the climate allows for nearly all types of sport, lazy beach lounging has been joined by plenty of other options for a fitness holiday. To start you off, here are two addresses of interest to sporty types looking for thrills, such as climbing, caving and cave-diving, or speed-boating: *www.mondaventura.com* and INSIDER TIP *www.escullaventura.com*.

BALLOONING

Grey-blue mountains, the silver-blue sea and the green of the trees on Mallorca's red earth – just approaching the island by plane makes your heart beat faster. If you want to relive these impressions in a more relaxed atmosphere, lift off from:

MALLORCA BALLOONS
Hot-air balloon adventures start in the early morning when there's no wind One hour of INSIDER TIP unhurried drifting at an altitude of 150–500 m costs 150 euros *(March–Oct)*. Boo kings (a week in advance!) / through *Mallorca Balloons (Carretera Palma-Manacor, km 44.4 | tel. 9 71 59 69 69 | www.mallorcaballoons.com)*.

Saddle up, dive in, lift off: Mallorca offers far more than lazy beach life; the island is ideal for a fitness holiday too

CYCLING

Inspired by the Olympic gold and bronze medals won by local track cyclist Joan Llaneras and by Tour de France winner Alberto Contador, the number of locals crossing the island's passes in colourful outfits on their sporty bikes increases year by year. In the winter season they are joined by some 70,000 holiday cyclists. In a bid to promote sustainable tourism, the island government has set up a 250 km network of cycle paths be-tween Campanet and Campos. There's no need to bring your own bike: bike hire is available in all resorts, with the options ranging from a simple touring bike *(trekking or mountainbike | around 9 euros per day)* to veritable racing machines *(day rate around 15 euros)*. The hotels *Delta* at Cala Blava, *Playa de Muro* and *Alcúdia Park* in the north are completely geared towards cyclists and run guided cycle trekking weeks. The best time of the year for cyclists is late September to early June.

A ride on the beach: the dream of many horse lovers comes true here

DIVING

Good scuba spots can be found in the northeast at Cala Sant Vicenç *(www. atemrausch.com)* and in the southwest, where the *Scuba Activa* diving base *(tel. 9 71 23 9102 | www.scuba-activa.com)* in Sant Elm offers beginners' courses with two dives for 269 euros. Also available are INSIDERTIP cave, wreck and night dives, mainly in the Isla Dragonera area.

GOLF

Boasting 21 playable courses, Mallorca has turned itself into a new European golfing mecca these days. Environ-mentalists reckon that 21 are too many, citing the issue of irrigation and the increased use of pesticides. There's space for more, counter the operators, pointing to regulations stipulating that new courses may only be sprinkled with treated used water. In any case: building continues. Three to four new courses are planned over the coming years. Save a lot on money on your golfing holiday with the Mallorca Golfcard for 99 euros *(www.mallorca-golfcard.com)*.

HIKING

As nearly all paths on the island lead through private property it makes sense to join an organised group, or at least get hold of one of the many hiking guides in book form. There has been a lot of progress in the signposting of official hiking trails and in extending the network of refuges; eleven of them are already accessible.

HORSERIDING

Cantering along the edge of the sea is a dream harboured by many. The *Ranchos* or *Clubs Hípic* set up in nearly every tourist centre help to make the dream come true. As the island is almost entirely in private hands and has many fences, it is best to join a guided hack. Toni Barceló's *Son Menut* horse riding centre in Felanitx hires out Andalusian stallions to experienced riders *(day hack 105 euros, 1 hr 16.50 euros | Camí de Son Negre | www. sonmenut.com)*. At the finca-turned-sports-hotel *Predio Son Serra* in Can Picafort all the action revolves around horseriding weeks and classes.

INLINE SKATING

Skating aces have established their own tracks in Palma: one running parallel to the harbour promenade from Porto Pi to El Molinar for a good 5 km, as well as one along the 12 km beach promenade of Platja de Palma. Here, holidaymakers mingle with Mallorcan youth.

KITESURFING

Fly over the waves with board and kite – kitesurfing is hot, not least on Mallorca. Advanced kitesurfers appreciate the bays of Palma and Alcúdia, whilst beginners will find better conditions at the bay of Es Trenc – or the Bahía de Pollença, where a mobile kitesurf school offers courses for beginners and advanced kitesurfers; beginners' course 60 euros, complete course 200 euros.

Tel. 6 05 19 66 29 | www.kitemallorca. com.

SAILING

Over 40 marinas, usually constant winds in summer and few drastic weather changes make the sea around the island an excellent sailing area. Fast skippers manage to round the island in one week. All larger ports offer chartered yachts (10-metre yacht from 1750 euros in the main season). The oldest and largest sailing school on the island (and in the Med) is Sail & Surf in Port de Pollença with a range of classes from a beginners course (265 euros) all the way to a week-long cruise around the island (625 euros including captain's dinner).

TENNIS

Mallorcan tennis ace Rafael Nadal, the former world number one, has made his sport very popular on the island. These days hardly a hotel worth its salt can afford to have no tennis court. One of the best facilities on the island, *Tennis Center Peguera,* is also one of the largest. Here the *Tennis Academy Mallorca* offers classes for beginners and master players, court fee 13 euros/hr, *Carrer Joaquim Blume, s/n | tel. 9 71 68 77 16 | www.tennisacademymallorca.com*

WINDSURFING

The same school also offers windsurfing courses *(beginners' course 265 euros)*; 40 boards are available. One of the best areas for the sport, the circular bay of Pollença, boasts excellent thermal winds. Other good areas for windsurfers are the bays of Cala Millor, Palma and Es Trenc, where you can also hire boards or take windsurfing lessons.

TRAVEL WITH KIDS

A child's smile is all it takes to brighten up the face of a disgruntled waiter or a stressed hotel maid: Spain is a very child-friendly country.

Flat sandy beaches and small coves, a back country with over a dozen leisure and nature parks, countless sports facilities and a well-maintained network of roads for trips by hire car make Mallorca one of the top destinations for family holidays in the Med.

Add to this child-friendly menus in restaurants, excellent medical care and a range of goods virtually indistinguishable from the ones back home. Even the late Spanish meal times don't need to create headaches for parents: for one, there is now a huge range of self-catering accommodation, apartments and country houses, secondly, most restaurant owners have changed their routines and open their doors early to foreign guests.

THE NORTH

BINIFALDÓ (140 A3) *(∅ J3)*

Keep the kids happy by combining a driving trip to Lluc monastery to listen to the choir boys singing with a INSIDER TIP ▶ picnic at Binifaldó, one of the island's best-equipped picnic spots: grill racks for a barbecue, tables and benches, toilets and a playground in a magnificent high mountain landscape; a great area for clambering around, and not only for

Take the plunge on the Devil's Tail: watery fun and exciting destinations for parents with children of all ages

the little ones. *Carretera Pollença–Lluc at km 17*

CAN PLANES (145 E1) *(ꕥ E4)*

This beautiful arts centre houses a collection of over 3000 historic toys: admire old doll's houses in Mallorcan style, nostalgic trains and cars. *Sa Pobla Carrer Antoni Maura 6 | Tue–Sat 10am–2pm and 4–8pm, Sun 10am–2pm | adults 3 euros, children go free*

FUNDACIÓN YANNICK AND BEN JAKOBER (141 D3) *(ꕥ M2)*

The neo-Moorish finca of *Sa Bassa Blanca* houses a unique private charitable foundation. Look out for the **INSIDER TIP** 150 historic children's portraits and a magnificent rose garden. *Mal Pas near Alcúdia | Wed–Sat guided tours | booking tel. 9 71 54 98 80 | www. fundacionjakober.org | admission 9–15 euros, children up to 10 go free*

THE EAST

FOOTBALL ACADEMY RUDI VÖLLER
(147 E5) *(ሥ P7)*

Under the guidance of trainers selected by German football legend Rudi Völler kids and adolescents can use their holidays in Cala Millor to improve their ball skills; after this, they'll be streets ahead once they're back home! Divided into age groups, students follow practical exercises five days a week, two hours a day. A five-day course costs 169 euros. Naturally, girls can play too! And on a Friday the dads take on the trainers. *On the country road from Cala Millor to Portocristo, behind the petrol station at the Club Monte Safari (signposted) | www.ca lamillor.org*

THE SOUTH

CALA FIGUERA (151 D5) *(ሥ N11)*

Leisure water parks are not the only option: the jetties in the protected harbour of Cala Figuera as well as the cliffs on the beaches of the south-eastern coast are a fabulous hunting ground for budding explorers: equipped with a bucket and dip net, they can try to catch or feed small fish, look for crabs, shells or pretty stones – whatever takes their fancy.

CALA SANTANYÍ (151 D5) *(ሥ M11)*

Hire a pedal boat at the beach and make your way around the right hand side of the rocky outcrop to discover and cruise through Es *Pontas,* a huge rock arch jutting up dramatically from the sea.

THE CENTRE

NATURA PARC SANTA EUGÈNIA ☺
(144 C4) *(ሥ H6)*

This nicely laid-out park full of animals and plants gives you a chance to see more or less all the assorted animal life on Mallorca, plus exotic creatures such as Maras and llamas. *Toca Toca* (tocar: to touch) is the name given to the children's petting zoo. *Kilometre 15.4 on the Palma–Sineu road (signposted) | www. naturaparc.net | Mon–Fri 10am–6/7pm, Sat/Sun 10am–8pm | adults 9 euros, children 6 euros*

PALMA AND THE WEST

GOLF FANTASIA (143 D5) *(ሥ D8)*

Boasting 54 holes, the mini-golf course in Palma Nova is one of the largest on the island. Beautifully laid out with subtropical plants, wooden bridges leading across gurgling brooks, artificial waterfalls, a duck pond and a café. At night the park is nicely illuminated. In fairness, some children might find 54 obstacles a bit too much; in which case, you may play only 18 holes – at a discount. *Carrer Tenis 3, next to the Palma Nova Palace Hotel | March–Oct daily 10am–midnight, outside the main season Mon–Wed and Fri–Sun 10.30am–6pm | adults 12.90 euros, children 7.50 euros | www.golffantasia.es*

HOUSE OF KATMANDU
(143 D5) *(ሥ D8)*

The latest family fun, set up following an American model, is a colourfully painted house in the Tibetan style, which stands on its head, and is haunted, but not only that. Eight darkened rooms full of surprises use acoustic and optical stimuli to take visitors from the torture chamber to the Yeti. New: a **INSIDER TIP** 4D cinema with two eight-minute animated films. Definitely not for scaredy-cats! *Magaluf | Avenida Pedro Vaquer Ramis 9 | at the Magaluf Park Hotel | www.houseofkatmandu.com | in summer daily 10am–midnight | adults 15.90 euros, children*

9.90 euros (with cinema 17.90 and 12.90 euros).

MARINELAND (143 D5) (*m D8*)

Shows featuring sea animals and parrots, an aquarium and a terrarium with exotic animals, a playground, ball park and a motor rally for kids. A highlight is the dolphin show which is shown several times daily. *Portals Nous | in summer daily 9.30am–4.45pm | adults 22.50 euros, children 16 euros*

INSIDER TIP ▶ PALMA AQUARIUM ●
(148 C3) (*m G8*)

Opened in 2007, this complex shelters 55 fish tanks with an impressive plant life and 8000 specimens from the world's oceans, a jungle landscape, a Mediterranean garden, restaurant and café. The transparent tunnel lets you get really close to the fish – and the sharks too...

Platja de Palma | motorway exit no. 10 (at Balneario 14, signposted) | www.palmaaquarium.com | daily 10am to 6pm (admission up to 5pm) | adults 19.50 euros, children 15 euros

PARC AVENTUR PUIGPUNYENT
(142 C3) (*m C6*)

Adventure park in the *Reserva de Galatzó* featuring wobbly rope bridges, daring scrambles, great slides and darts. *5 km outside Puigpunyent (signposted) | www.lareservaaventur.com | daily 10am–5pm | adults and children (who have to be at least 8 years of age) 26.50 euros.* Visitors who only want to hike through the Reserva's nature park pay 12.50 euros (adults) and 6.25 euros (children). Admission for both parks: *adults 39 euros, children 32.75 euros.* The parks are closed between mid-December and mid-February.

Pulling in the crowds: dolphin show in Marineland, Portals Nous

FESTIVALS & EVENTS

In Palma, they might call it an 'event', but the villages simply call it a *festa* (feast) or *fira* (Mass). And now as then the island's annual cycle of events is guided by the calendar of the Catholic church. Every community celebrates its patron saint for a whole week. Year on year though, folklore traditions are giving way to more modern sounds. Today, hard-rock bands and *botellons* (youth groups bringing their own booze) are as much part of the festival atmosphere as the *xeremiers* traditional minstrel groups. In the capital of Palma in particular, there is a steady stream of festivities (for dates, consult the island's English-language weekly magazines).

PUBLIC HOLIDAYS

1 Jan *Cap d'any*, New Year; **6 Jan** *Els Reis Mags*, Epiphany; **1 March** *Dia de les Illes Balears*, Balearic regional holiday; **March/April** *Divendres Sant*, Good Friday; **1 May** *Festa del Traball*, Labour Day; **25 July** *Sant Jaume*, St James' Day; **15 Aug** *L'Assumpció*, Assumption of the Virgin; **12 Oct** *Dia de l'Hispanitat*, Discovery of America Day; **1 Nov** *Tots Sants*, All Saints; **6**

Dec *Dia de la Constitució*, Constitution Day; **8 Dec** *La Immaculada Concepció*, Immaculate Conception; **25/26 Dec** *Nadal*, Christmas

FESTIVALS & EVENTS

JANUARY

16 Jan, ▶ *Eve of Sant Antoni:* spectacle in sa Pobla, where ▶ *dimonis* (devils) roam the streets, dotted with burning ▶ *fogerós* (pyres)

20 Jan, ▶ *Sant Sebastià:* a week of festivities in Palma; on the eve of the day there is live music on all major squares and giant firework displays above the port.

MARCH/APRIL

▶ *Semana Santa/Pasqua:* At 7pm on Maundy Thursday a procession starts in Palma. 30 confraternities with pointed hats and face masks carry statues of the Virgin Mary and Christ. On Good Friday, for ▶ *Devallament*, confraternities from Pollença carry a statue of Christ down Calvary into the church.

APRIL

In mid-April, dancers and musicians from over 30 countries give their best

Processions, concerts, festivals: nearly all Mallorcan festivities have a religious origin

for the ▶ *World Folklore Festival*, with processions and shows on Palma's larger squares.

MAY

Early May: ▶ *Fira del Disc,* pop music fair in Palma's trade fair centre
From 2nd Sunday ▶ *Feria* in Sóller; Monday afternoon ▶ *moros i cristians:* Moors and Christians recreate a battle that took place in 1561.

JUNE

Early June: ▶ *International Jazz Festival* in Cala d'Or
▶ *El Corpus,* Corpus Christi: two beautifully decked-out girls in eagle costumes take the lead at the ▶ *Processó de les Aguiles* procession in Pollença.
29 June: ▶ *Sant Pere i Sant Paul,* in honour of the apostles Peter and Paul, a colourful boat procession takes place in Port d'Alcúdia, Port d'Andratx and Port de Sóller.

JULY/AUGUST

▶ *Music festivals* are staged in Valldemossa (Chopin), at Bellver Castle in Palma (Summer Serenades), in Deià/Son Marroig (chamber music) and in the Santo Domingo monastery in Pollença (featuring soloists of world renown); for exact dates, check the island's English-language press.
In late July over 200 singers and dancers perform at the ▶ *International Folklore Festival* in Sóller.
28 July: ▶ *Cavalcada de la Beateta* ('the little blessed one') in Valldemossa: a girl from the village represents the island's saint Catalina Tomàs in a solemn procession.
2 Aug: the battle between ▶ *moros i cristians* as the culmination of the ▶ *festival of the patron saint of Pollença* (7pm on the Rooster Fountain) seems impressively realistic.
15 Aug: ▶ INSIDER TIP ▶ massive firework display with music above the harbour of Can Picafort for the end of the ▶ *Virgen del Carmen* fiesta.

LINKS, BLOGS, APPS & MORE

LINKS

▶ www.gotomallorca.net/guiasvirtuales/lacatedral/1.html This impressive virtual guide through Palma's La Seu Cathedral starts with an overview of the outside. Clicking on the Miniaturas button (top right) yields 360° images of the entire nave, the main altar with the Gaudí chandelier and the huge ceramic mural by Miquel Barcel; the accompanying text is in Spanish and English

▶ www.bestmallorcawalks.co.uk Does what it says on the tin! This site provides comprehensive information on a selection of tried and tested hiking trails in all parts of the island, safety precautions, links and much more

BLOGS & FORUMS

▶ http://obcn.wordpress.com/tag/flor-de-sal-des-trenc/ Fine photos of various subjects by Santanyí-based photographer Oliver Brenneisen, amongst them the Flor de Sal salt extraction in Ses Salines

▶ www.digamemallorca.com/blog.html Up-to-date guide to cultural, gastronomic and touristic events from Mallorca's acclaimed listings magazine

▶ http://mallorcaphotoblog.wordpress.com/ A photographic homage to Mallorca, updated daily – or near enough

VIDEOS

▶ www.youtube.com/watch?v=KhdNaxwnpzg A declaration of love on video: Javier Pierotti's ,I love Mallorca' offers beautiful images of the island, nicely put

Regardless of whether you are still preparing your trip or already in Mallorca: these addresses will provide you with more information, videos and networks to make your holiday even more enjoyable.

together with equally beautiful music (length: 4 min 33 sec)

▶ www.mallorca-movies.com/der-toilettenmann/ In Cala Rajada's Bolero club not even the men's toilets offer peace and quiet – this is where `the loo man' entertains a loyal following

▶ www.youtube.com/watch?v=K6d8aqJYVtc Mallorca's anthem ‚La Balanguera', sung with gusto by the Mallorcan chanson singer Maria del Mar Bonet (4 mins 31 sec)

▶ www.youtube.com/watch?v=af0_R1g1AjU This 10-minute video on the aquarium in Palma really makes you feel like paying a visit to the fish

▶ www.youtube.com/watch?v=94xyOpETYYs&feature=related Several outtakes in front of a rolling camera feature Mallorcan native Rafael Nadal and Roger Federer promoting their *Match for Africa* (3 mins 18 sec) – broken up again and again by infectious laughter

▶ www.englishradiomallorca.com 92.9 Up-to-date news, music and weather forecasts in English; free

▶ Mallorca essentials island guide with ten selected trips, visits to ten island villages, 15 beaches and 250 useful addresses for visitors. 60 video clips available on youtube; most users have given this app a good rating

▶ www.majorca.info/blog-about-majorca Mallorca holidaymakers helping each other, including photos and virtual tours

▶ www.booking.com/hotel Useful hotel reviews by real travellers (enter ‚Mallorca')

▶ www.mallorca-beaches.com/ Let's face it: beaches is what most people visit Mallorca for. This handy illustrated site lists them for you

TRAVEL TIPS

ACCOMMODATION RESERVATIONS

Hotel rooms booked through travel operators are usually cheaper, all-inclusive offers in particular. The downside of this is that hardly any private accommodation is on offer, making spur-of-the-moment trips a bit tricky. Between May and October you will have great difficulty to find a place to stay of your choice at short notice.

The following sites are useful addresses for finding accommodation:
www.hotels.com/Mallorca
www.specialplacestostay.com
www.theothermallorca.com.
Fincas can be arranged through many English and German tour operators, or also the *Associació de Agroturisme Balear* in Palma *(tel. 9 71 72 15 08 | www.topfincas.com).*

RESPONSIBLE TRAVEL

It doesn't take a lot to be environmentally friendly whilst travelling. Don't just think about your carbon footprint whilst flying to and from your holiday destination but also about how you can protect nature and culture abroad. As a tourist it is especially important to respect nature, look out for local products, cycle instead of driving, save water and much more. If you would like to find out more about eco-tourism please visit: *www. ecotourism.org*

ARRIVAL

Driving to Mallorca from London involves about 1100 km of motorway driving, via Orleans – Bourges – Clermond-Ferrand – Millau to Barcelona. Toll charges in France and Spain: about 100 euros.

The green choice: letting the train take the strain is possible if time-consuming. Travel time from London to Barcelona on sleeper or daytime trains is about 15 hours. Depending on the season, a regular second-class return ticket from London starts from around 260 euros. *www.seat61.com* is an excellent site for timetables and ticketing links. Keep an eye out for special offers!

International flights touch down at Palma de Mallorca (Son Sant Joan airport). Flight time from London is under 2.5 hours, and Palma is served by most UK regional airports. The majority of holidaymakers uses the charter flight offers (expect to pay between 100 and 300 euros). Economy-class scheduled flights with BA or Iberia range between 200 and 500 euros. The cheapest option (starting at 40 euros) are seasonal special offers, easyjet, as well as booking well in advance. Several hire-car firms tout for business at the airport; taxis offer transfers to the island's other regions and towns. The longest trip, to Cala Rajada, costs about 90 euros; travelling into the centre of Palma costs around 25 euros by taxi, against 1.80 euros by bus.

The Trasmediterránea *(www.trasmediterranea.com)* Barcelona-Palma

From arrival to weather

Holiday from start to finish: the most important addresses and information for your Mallorca trip

de Mallorca car ferry runs daily, in summer several times a day, and takes eight hours. Prices per car in high season hover around 180 euros, and 120 euros for a double cabin (including port tax)

BANKS & MONEY

Practically all towns on the island have several banks, and there are few places without an ATM cash machine. Daily limit for withdrawals per credit card 300–500 euros.

BUSES & TRAINS

The underground bus and railway station in Palma, below the park opposite Plaça Espanya, is called Estació Intermodal. This is where the trains to/from Inca-Muro-sa Pobla and all overland buses to/from all towns on the island leave from. There is an information point with English-speaking staff. Tickets can be bought from the driver.

The railway station also houses a bike hire facility – apart from the historic quarter and in the entirely pedestrianised areas, a bike is not a bad way to get around Palma, and green to boot!

Opposite the railway hotel you will find the Art Nouveau railway station serving the nostalgic *Ferrocarril de Sóller*. Modern trains connect Palma with Inca, sa Pobla and Manacor. It is planned to extend the rail network from sa Pobla to Alcúdia and from Manacor to Cala Rajada. Otherwise, there are precious few connections between the towns on the island; everything centres around Palma.

CAMPING

Mallorca is no island for campers: there are no campsites. At the Lluc monastery *(tel. 971 87 15 25)* camping for one night

BUDGETING

Taxi	0.95 euros *per kilometre in Palma*
Coffee	from 1.20 euros *for an espresso coffee*
Beach	about 7–10 euros *for two recliners with parasol*
Tapas	from 3.50 euros *for a small portion*
Petrol	1.20 euros *for one litre of petrol*
Ice cream	from 1.20 euros *for a scoop*

is sometimes possible, on request and as an exception only.

CAR HIRE

Hundreds of car-hire companies offer around 35,000 rental cars. Check and contrast the terms: particularly cheap offers aren't necessarily the most trustworthy. It is worth taking out fully comprehensive insurance with no excess in case of damage. A hire car of the lower category costs about 175 euros a week excluding petrol – when you book from home that is. Generally hire cars booked over the internet from home (from and to the airport) are a lot cheaper than those rented on a whim in holiday centres.

CLIMATE, WHEN TO GO

The north is cooler than the south. Spring is usually mild with cool evenings and rain showers. Summers are hot with occasional thunder and lightning, August has high levels of humidity. Autumn stays warm well into October, after that the first cold spells arrive, and with them a lot of precipitation. Winters are predominantly mild, and due to high humidity in the evening and at night turn cool to cold.

CONSULATES AND EMBASSIES

BRITISH CONSULATE
Palma, Carrer Convent dels Caputxins | 4 Edificio Orisba B 4º | tel. 9 02 10 93 56 | Mon–Fri 8.30am–1.30pm | http://ukin spain.fco.gov.uk/en

IRISH CONSULATE GENERAL
Palma, San Miguel, 68 | tel. 9 71 72 25 04

US CONSULATE AGENCY
Palma, Porto Pi, 8 | tel. 9 71 40 37 07

CUSTOMS

EU citizens can import and export goods for their personal use tax-free (800 cigarettes, 1 kg tobacco, 90 l of wine, 10 l of spirits over 22 %).

Visitors from other countries must observe the following limits, except for items for personal use. Duty free are: max. 50 g perfume, 200 cigarettes, 50 cigars, 250 g tobacco, 1 L of spirits (over 22 % vol.), 2 L of spirits (under 22 % vol.), 2 L of any wine.

DRIVING

Apart from driving on the right-hand side of the road, traffic regulations are broad-ly similar to the UK. Maximum speed limits on motorways: 120 km/h (75 mph); on country roads: 90 km/h (55 mph). Seat belts have to be worn at all times; and a helmet must be worn on all motorised two-wheel vehicles. Blood alcohol limit: 0.5. Carrying a fluorescent vest is compulsory, and using a mobile phone whilst driving is prohibited. Penalties *(multas)* are very high. In villages and towns, blue lines pinpoint limited and payable parking, yellow ones signal no parking. Ignore parking restrictions at your peril unless you want to pay *multas* or have your car towed away. In the centre of Palma machines sell pay and display tickets for up to 90 minutes maximum.

EMERGENCY

European emergency number (police, fire service, ambulance): *tel. 112*

FOREST FIRES

There isn't that much forest on Mallorca in the first place. Which is why forest fires, often occurring after extended periods of hot weather and drought, can have a dramatic impact. Alongside pyromaniacs and lightning striking, carelessness and negligence are the biggest factors. Don't ever throw a cigarette butt out of a driving car, don't leave any glass bottles lying around and don't start a barbecue in the forest – many public picnic spots ban barbecues altogether!

HEALTH

The island has a comprehensive network of doctors' surgeries (you'll find addresses of English-speaking medics in the Majorca Daily Bulletin available from news stands) and pharmacies *(far-*

macias). There are also eleven private and ten state-run hospitals (providing interpreters). Over a dozen alternative medicine services have settled on Mallorca. The holiday resorts have their own *centros médicos,* and the Red Cross *(Cruz Roja)* provides first aid on many beaches. Medical emergencies (island-wide, around the clock) *Red Cross: tel. 9 71 20 22 22*

IMMIGRATION

A valid passport is required for entry into Spain. All children must travel with their own passport.

INFORMATION

SPANISH TOURIST OFFICE
UK: 79 New Cavendish Street, London W1A 6NB | tel. 00 800 1010 5050 | www. spain.info
US: Los Angeles, Miami, New York, Chicago
Canada: Toronto Tourist Office of Spain | 2 Bloor Streets West 34th Floor, Toronto, Ontario | tel. 14 16 / 96 13 131 – 96 14 0 79

INTERNET

Typing 'Mallorca' into a search engine will yield around 52 million results. Amongst the websites of interest to holidaymakers are *www.mallorca.com* with up-to-date not specifically tourism-related information; *www.vivamallorca. com* is a very useful site for travellers, clear and well-structured; *www.spain. info* is the official homepage of the Spanish tourist office, featuring useful information for preparing your trip. A factual search engine for anybody interested in the island is *www.mallorcaweb. com* and a further source of online information is *www.seemallorca.com.*

Travellers looking for a travel buddy can try *www.travbuddy.com.*

INTERNET CAFÉS & WIFI

A reliable internet café in Palma's here-there-gone-tomorrow scene is Azul Contact *Cyber Café | Mon–Fri 10am–9pm, Sat/Sun 10am–8pm | Carrer Soledad 4 | tel. 9 71 71 29 27 | 50 cents for the connection and 3 cents per minute.* For further addresses on the island check *www.ccpalma.com/ internet/cybercafe.html.* WiFi (Wireless Fidelity) is not yet available across the entire island. More and more hotels though are getting WiFi installed, and entire regions, such as the coast of Calvià, the beach of

CURRENCY CONVERTER

£	€	€	£
1	1.10	1	0.90
3	3.30	3	2.70
5	5.50	5	4.50
13	14.30	13	11.70
40	44	40	36
75	82.50	75	67.50
120	132	120	108
250	275	250	225
500	550	500	450

$	€	€	$
1	0.70	1	1.40
3	2.10	3	4.20
5	3.50	5	7
13	9.10	13	18.20
40	28	40	56
75	52.50	75	105
120	84	120	168
250	175	250	350
500	350	500	700

For current exchange rates see www.xe.com

Port d'Alcúdia and the old jetty including Parc de la Mar in Palma offer this service.

A list of all Balearic marinas, with information on location, size, number of moorings, maximum length of boats allowed and port facilities, as well as of all providers of charter yachts, can be obtained from *Mallorca nautic | Carrer Joan Miró 20 | 07014 Palma de Mallorca | tel. 9 71 28 00 07 | www.mallorcanautic.com*. The only agency on the Balearics listing all charter companies (over 80) describes all available boat types on its website and can also arrange skippers for about 135 euros per day.

MEDIA

Nearly all hotels offer British and other English-language TV programmes via satellite. News stands sell British newspapers, as well as the English-language daily, weekly and monthly papers and magazines, such as Majorca Daily Bulletin, Digame, or Mallorca Life & Style. The English-language island radio *(www.englishradiomallorca.com)* broadcasts *Sat/Sun 10am–1pm on 92.9FM Radio Marratxi.*

OPENING HOURS

Restaurants are usually open *1–4pm and 7.30–11pm,* shops on weekdays

WEATHER IN MALLORCA

	Jan	Feb	March	April	May	June	July	Aug	Sept	Oct	Nov	Dec
Daytime temperatures in °C/°F												
	14/57	15/59	17/63	19/66	23/73	27/81	29/84	30/86	27/81	23/73	18/64	15/59
Nighttime temperatures in °C/°F												
	6/43	6/43	7/45	9/48	13/55	16/61	19/66	19/66	18/64	14/57	10/50	7/45
Sunshine hours/day												
	5	6	6	7	10	10	11	11	8	6	5	5
Precipitation days/month												
	6	6	6	4	4	2	1	2	5	6	7	7
Water temperature in °C/°F												
	14/57	13/55	14/57	15/59	17/63	21/70	24/75	25/77	24/75	21/70	18/64	15/59

9am–1/1.30pm and 4–8.30pm and longer.

PHONE & MOBILE PHONE

Using the hotel telephone is very expensive. If you are using a payphone (blue-green) bring a phone card, available from tobacco and souvenir shops from 5 euros (including approx. 10 minutes speaking time). For calls outside Spain dial 00 followed by the dialling code for the country (UK 44, Ireland 353, US and Canada 1) and of the town/city (without the 0), then the number of the person you are calling. The code for Spain is 0034. The biggest provider of mobile phone services is Telefónica, followed by Uni-2 and Retevisión.

Yachts in Port de Portals

POST

Stamps can be bought from the post office *(correos)* and in the tobacco shops *(tabaco, estanco)*. Letterboxes are yellow. Post stamped with private firms' stamps will only be collected from that particular company's letterbox!

PRICES

Fruit and vegetables are often more expensive on markets than in the supermarkets without being necessarily fresher! Fresh meat continues to be good value, but not fresh fish, as it has become rare here too. Tourists complain about high prices in restaurants – rightly so in many places, especially as prices often seem to bear little relation to the quality. A bottle of table wine costing some 2.50 euros in the supermarket can cost 15 times as much in a restaurant. Organised trips are also a drain on holiday finances: 30–65 euros for a day excursion without packed lunch or a show evening with a set menu.

TIPPING

Anybody working in the service industry is glad of a tip. In restaurants, it is customary to add up to 10 per cent to the total bill. Maids expect 5–6 euros per week. The charge for taxis or private coach transport should be rounded up generously, and guides usually receive a gratuity of around 5–10 euros or more if you were happy with the service.

WATER

Even after the construction of the desalination plants near Palma and the deployment of mobile desalination units, the potable water supply remains a problem in Mallorca, especially in years with little rain. In high summer the drinking water in many coastal areas becomes very salty. Also, the island consists of limestone, making the water very hard. The best thing to do is to drink only mineral water and restrict water use to essential needs.

USEFUL PHRASES CATALAN

PRONUNCIATION

c	like "s" before "e" and "i" (e.g. Barcelona); like "k" before "a", "o" and "u" (e.g. Casa)
ç	pronounced like "s" (e.g. França)
g	like "s" in "pleasure" before "e" and "i"; like "g" in "get" before "a", "o" and "u"
l·l	pronounced like "l"
que/qui	the "u" is always silent, so "qu" sounds like "k" (e.g. perquè)
v	at the start of a word and after consonants like "b" (e.g. València)
x	like "sh" (e.g. Xina)

IN BRIEF

Yes/No/Maybe	Sí/No/Potser
Please/Thank you/Sorry	Sisplau/Gràcies/ Perdoni
May I ...?	Puc ...?
Pardon?	Com diu *(Sie)*?/Com dius *(Du)*?
I would like to .../	Voldria .../
Have you got ...?	Té ...?
How much is ...?	Quant val ...?
I (don't) like this	(no) m'agrada
good	bo/bé *(Adverb)*
bad	dolent/malament *(Adverb)*
Help!/Attention!/Caution!	Ajuda!/Compte!/Cura!
ambulance	ambulància
police/fire brigade	policia/bombers
Prohibition/forbidden	prohibició/prohibit
danger/dangerous	perill/perillós
May I take a photo here/of you?	Puc fer-li una foto aquí?

GREETINGS, FAREWELL

Good morning!/afternoon!	Bon dia!
Good evening!/night!	Bona tarda!/Bona nit!
Hello!/Goodbye!	Hola!/Adéu! Passi-ho bé!
See you	Adéu!
My name is ...	Em dic ...
What's your name?	Com es diu?

Parles Català?

"Do you speak Catalan?" This guide will help you to say the basic words and phrases in Catalan.

DATE & TIME

Monday/Tuesday	dilluns/dimarts
Wednesday/Thursday	dimecres/dijous
Friday/Saturday	divendres/dissabte
Sunday/working day	diumenge/dia laborable
holiday	dia festiu
today/tomorrow/	avui/demà/
yesterday	ahir
hour/minute	hora/minut
day/night/week	dia/nit/setmana

TRAVEL

open/closed	obert/tancat
entrance/driveway	entrada
exit/exit	sortida
departure/	sortida/
departure/arrival	sortida d'avió/arribada
toilets/restrooms /	Lavabos/
ladies/gentlemen	Dones/Homes
Where is ...?/	On està ...?/
Where are ...?	On estan ...?
left/right	a l'esquerra/a la dreta
close/far	a prop/lluny
bus	bus
taxi/cab	taxi
bus stop/	parada/
cab stand	parada de taxis
parking lot/	aparcament/
parking garage	garatge
street map/map	pla de la ciutat/mapa
train station/harbour	estació/port
airport	aeroport
schedule/ticket	horario/bitllet
train / platform/track	tren/via
platform	andana
I would like to rent ...	Voldria llogar ...
a car/a bicycle	un cotxe/una bicicleta
petrol/gas station	gasolinera
petrol/gas / diesel	gasolina/gasoil
breakdown/repair shop	avaria/taller

FOOD & DRINK

Could you please book a table for tonight for four?	Voldriem reservar una taula per a quatre persones per avui al vespre
on the terrace	a la terrassa
The menu, please	la carta, sisplau
Could I please have ...?	Podria portar-me ...?
bottle/carafe/glass	ampolla/garrafa/got
salt/pepper/sugar	sal/pebrot/sucre
vinegar/oil	vinagre/oli
vegetarian/	vegetarià/vegetariana/
allergy	allèrgia
May I have the bill, please?	El compte, sisplau

SHOPPING

Where can I find...?	On hi ha ...?
I'd like .../	voldria/
I'm looking for ...	estic buscant ...
pharmacy/chemist	farmacia/drogueria
baker/market	forn/mercat
shopping center	centre comercial/gran magatzem
supermarket	supermercat
kiosk	quiosc
expensive/cheap/price	car/barat/preu
organically grown	de cultiu ecológic

ACCOMMODATION

I have booked a room	He reservat una habitació
Do you have any ... left?	Encara té ...
single room	una habitació individual
double room	una habitació doble
breakfast/half board	esmorzar/mitja pensió
full board	pensió completa
at the front/seafront	exterior/amb vistes al mar
shower/sit down bath	dutxa/bany
balcony/terrace	balcó/terrassa

BANKS, MONEY & CREDIT CARDS

bank/ATM	banc/caixer automàtic
pin code	codi secret
cash/	al comptat/
credit card	amb targeta de crèdit
change	canvi

HEALTH

doctor/dentist/paediatrician	metge/dentista/pediatre
hospital/emergency clinic	hospital/urgència
fever/pain	febre/dolor
inflamed/injured	inflamat/ferit
plaster/bandage	tireta/embenat
ointment/cream	pomada/crema
pain reliever/tablet	analgèsic/pastilla

POST, TELECOMMUNICATIONS & MEDIA

stamp/letter/postcard	segell/carta/ postal
I need a landline phone card	Necessito una targeta telefònica per la xarxa fixa
I'm looking for a prepaid card for my mobile	Estic buscant una targeta de prepagament pel mòbil
Where can I find internet access?	On em puc connectar a Internet?
Do I need a special area code?	He de marcar algun prefix determinat?
socket/adapter/charger	endoll/adaptador/carregador
computer/battery/ rechargeable battery	ordinador/bateria/ acumulador
at sign (@)	arrova
internet address	adreça d'internet (URL)
e-mail address	adreça de correu electrònic
e-mail/file/print	correu electrònic/fitxer/imprimir

LEISURE, SPORTS & BEACH

beach	platja
sunshade/lounger	para-sol/gandula

NUMBERS

0 zero	12 dotze	60 seixanta
1 un/una	13 tretze	70 setanta
2 dos/dues	14 catorze	80 vuitanta
3 tres	15 quinze	90 noranta
4 quatre	16 setze	100 cent
5 cinc	17 disset	200 dos-cents/dues-centes
6 sis	18 divuit	1000 mil
7 set	19 dinou	2000 dos mil
8 vuit	20 vint	10000 deu mil
9 nou	30 trenta	
10 deu	40 quaranta	½ mig
11 onze	50 cinquanta	¼ un quart

NOTES

MARCO POLO TRAVEL GUIDES

MARCO POLO

ROAD ATLAS & PULL-OUT MAP

KE GARDA

BALDO WITH MOUNTAIN BIKE
with Malcesine takes bikes too

SSES " IN SALO
ssate ..bacetti"

Travel with
Insider
Tips

MARCO POLO

With STREET ATLAS & PULL-OUT MAP

EW YORK

S, WILD FLOWERS AND SKYSCRAPERS
The High Line in Chelsea

IN CLOUD NINE
bar at 230 Fifth Street

Travel with
Insider
Tips

MARCO POLO

With STREET ATLAS & PULL-OUT MAP

FRENCH RIVIERA
NICE, CANNES & MONACO

SPECTACULAR GRAND CANYON DU VERDON
Breath-taking scenery that takes some beating

SNIFFING THE AIR
The perfume manufacturers of Grasse

Travel with
Insider
Tips

www.marcopolo.com

MARCO POLO

With STREET ATLAS & PULL-OUT MAP

BERLIN

A STUNNING ISLAND JUST FOR ART
Showcasing treasures from around the world

Y COOL AT NIGHT
rlin club scene sets the trend

Travel with
Insider
Tips

MARCO POLO

With ROAD ATLAS & PULL-OUT MAP

ALLORCA

X FLAIR IN THE MEDITERRANEAN
llorca's most beautiful beach

" IN" CROWD MEET
nda in Deia

Travel with
Insider
Tips

- PACKED WITH INSIDER TIPS
- BEST WALKS AND TOURS
- FULL-COLOUR PULL-OUT MAP
  AND STREET ATLAS

ROAD ATLAS

The green line ▬▬▬ indicates the Trips & Tours.
The blue line ▬▬▬ indicates the Perfect Route.

All tours are also marked on the pull-out map

Photo: Cala Figuera

Travelling around Mallorca

The map on the back cover shows how the area has been sub-divided

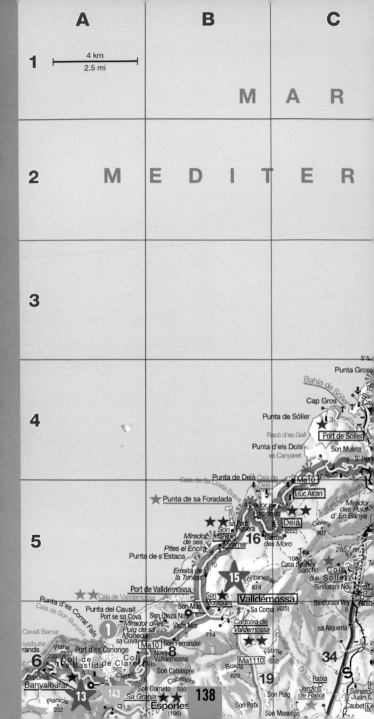

4 km
2.5 mi

M A R

M E D I T E R

S'Il

Punta Gross

Bahía de Sóller

Cap Gros

To
Sa
Ca

Punta de Sóller

Port de Sóller

Racó d'es Gall

Son Muleta

Punta d'els Dols

S' Hor

es Canyaret

Punta de Deià   Cala de

Cala de Sa Costa Brava   Deià

Ma10

Lluc Alcari

Punta de sa Foradada

Mirador de sa
Foradada

Deià
(222)

Mirador
des Pujol
d' En Banya

Galera
907

sa Font
Figuera
Son
Marroig

16

Mirador
de ses
Pites el Encira

Miramar

Castell
des Moro

Tex

2857 m

Punta de s'Estaca

10

Casa del Rey
Sancho

Coll
de Sóller

Ermita de
la Trinitat

15

Fontanells
874

Biniforani Nou

Port de Valldemossa

Son
Moragues

Valldemossa

Sa Coma (425)

Biniforani Vey

Jar
d

Arat

Punta d'es Corral Fals

Cala de Valldemossa

Punta del Cavall

Cala de Son Bunyola

Port se sa Cova

1

Mirador d'es
Moneda
sa Cova

Puig de sa

Son Oleza Nou

Vista Mar

Cartoixa de
Valldemossa

sa Alqueria

Cavall Bernat

Ma10

Son Ferrandel

714

Fàtima

34

nyalbufar

randa

Plana
433

290

Port d'es Canonge

Coll de
la Bastida

Nova
Valldemossa

8

Boxos
626

Ma1110   650

19

S

6

Coll
de Clares

562

Clares

495

Son Cabaspre

Cabaspre

Baronia

Banyalbufar

planicie
932

13

143

Son Dameto   593

Sa Granja

1.5

Esporles
(196)

138

Son Patx

Son Puig

Son Masellas

Raixa

Jardins
de Raixa

Sanato
t Juan M

Caubet
M

D E F

1

À N I A

Cova de

Fig

es Musclos de ses Cordes

Single d'es Pi
389
389
ses Bases

Corral d'en Figuera
es Morro d'en Llobera

es Puig Caragoler
920
798
Femenies Vell
Mont

Morro de sa Vaca
Cala d'es Capellans
Cala Codera

Morro del Bordils
Cala Tex

Cala de sa Vaca
Torre de Lluc
439

Puig Roig
1002

Cala de ses Fel·les
Racó de sa Corma
Mola de Tuent
459

sa Calobra

Cavall Bernat

sa Moleta
782

Coscona
843

Son Llobera
13,5

Mossa

Ma10

Son Alzines
Binifaldo

Morro d'es Forat
Cala Tuent
Església de Sant Llorenç

Entreforc

Son Colomi

Montes Manut
Aubarca

sa Moleta
825

Cala Rotja
Taleca
Racó de sa

12

sa Moleta
782

Escorca

Casa Nova

Lluc
753

Santuari de Monestir de Lluc

Torre sa Seca

Gorg d'es Dies

Ma2141

1,5

Puig Ferrer

Bini Petit

E s c o r c a

Balitx d'Abaix
d'es Lloss

Puig Major
1443

Serra d'es Teix

Coll de Sa Batalla

805
arques

3 2

Embalse de Gorg Blau

1345

Comafreda
4,5

Ma2130

Son Torrella

Macanella

Coma de Son Torella

Ma10

Barracar

Puig d'es Barracar
621

Fir
Es
Binibon

4

4

Fornalutx

880

Tossals
1047

es Tossals Vels
1103

5,5

19

Biniaraix
iuria
d'es Comte

Bini Morat

Embalse de Cuber

Caimari

Alfabia

Ofre
Comasema

Serra d'es Puig d'es Moix

Maçanella

Ma2131

Alfabia
1067

Son Vidal

Mola de Son Montserrat

Aumedrà

Sant Llorenç

Surd
641

Ma2114

Selva

Mancor de la Vall
(202)

Ma2112

Orient

Castell d'Alaró
746

Sollerich

622

Cova de Sant Antoni
816

Puig de Sa Creu
672

Soucadena

Biniamar

Oratori de Crist Rei

Ma2113

Ma2130

Inca

Ma2100

Son Verga
5,5

Torren

Lloseta
(152)

Ma2110

Santa

Son Fuster de Abais

Penya de Can
Jeroni
409

Ma2110

Son Pou
s'Avenc de Son Pou

Orient
uer

Alaró
(225)

Ma2022

Son Forteza

Son Borneta

Ermita es Coco

Can Canto

(1212)

(27)

Ferro de Mallorca

Ma3120

amarich
666

Es Cabas

4,5

La Mina

Son Antem

Ma2021

3

Binissalem
(137)

Ma2050

Ma13A

Can Negre
Aqua
Langia

Museu
Histórial

Ma13

5,5

Son

139

144

Son Mall Nou

2,5

Son Pontiró

2,5

Biniagual

Son Aloy

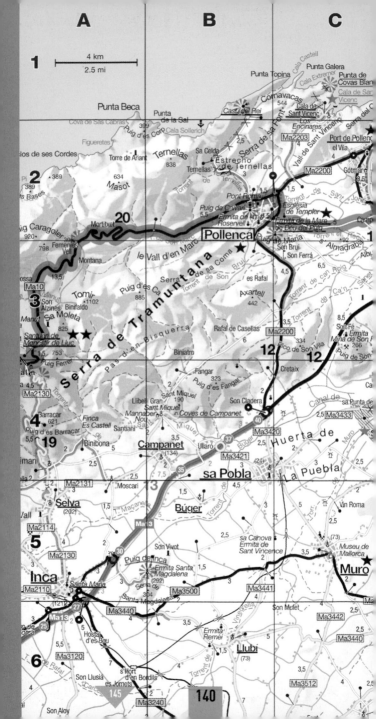

A

B

C

1

M A R
M E D I T E R R À N I A

2

★ *Torre Talaia de Ses Ànim*
Punta d' es Ven

Punta de Son Serralta

En

Cala Estellencs
Port de Estellencs
Cala Ca's Xeramie
Platja Can Prua **Coll d'es P**
Punta de sa Lluenta *Mirador de*
★★ *R. Roca* **35** Este

3

Punta de sa Foradada
es Grau
Serra d' es Pinotells
Cala de ses Ortigue Galatz
Punta de sa Llova ·926 1026
es Barraca Esclop
Descarregador ★
Fondal de *La Reserva Parc Natural*
Punta d'en Fabiolet ses Basses
Ma10
Morro Ratjada Bachas
SA DRAGONERA Cala **S** Caserio Galatzó
Parc Natural Basset *sa Trapa* **Coll de** s'Alqueria
de Dragonera 491 **sa Gremola**
Torre **Can Seriat** Grua
en Basset 422 482 · Son Mortolá
Punta Basset Abidale Son Boch 8.5
Negra Sant Elm 330 Son Guiem 5.5
310 Son Castell **Ma1081** Es
Dragonera Cala Lladó s'Arracó Sa Coma Capdell
4 I. PANTALEU **Ma1030** · Son Mas **Ma1031**
Cala Llebeitx Cala Conills Emita **Andratx** Son Alfonso
Cap Llebeitx *Castell* Antic **Ma1050** Carras Son Vich Nou
de Sant Elm Enrich 318 (139) Coll 461 **Ma1012**
Punta Galinda 276 **Ma1** d'Andritxol 125 Son Fortuny **12**
Cap Falcons Cala d'Antio Son Vich Tora
Cala d'Egos Port d'Andratx **Ma1** *Túnel de*
Punta Moragues *Sol Vich* **Ma1A** 840 m Peguera
Badia de Andratx 1.5 **Ma1020** Camp de Mar sa Romana
Can Inglés Platja Peguera Costa
Cala Raco *de Camp* Fomells **Ma1** Calma
★ **Cap de sa Mola** *de Mar* Cala Platja Costa
Cala Marmassén Fomells *de* de la Calma
Cala Llamp **Cap Andritxol** *Peguera*
Cap d' es Llamp Punta des Castellot 2.5
Ensenada Cala de Santa Ponca Santa
5 de Santa Ponça *sa Caleta* Son
Na Foradada 2.5
I. de los CONEJOS
I. MALGRATS
Punta Enguisa
Cala de Penyes Rojes el Toro

6
4 km
2.5 mi
Cala
Refeube
I. DEL TORO

142

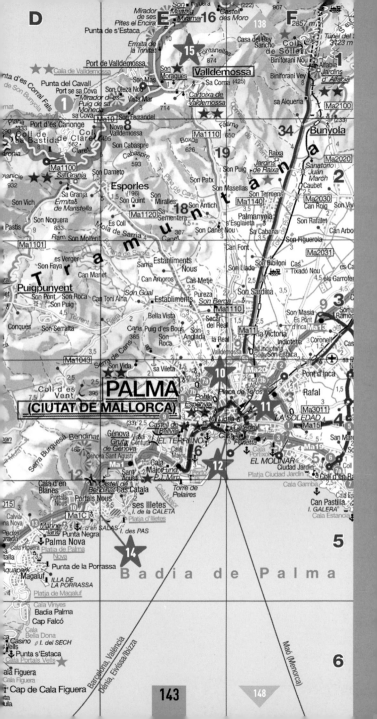

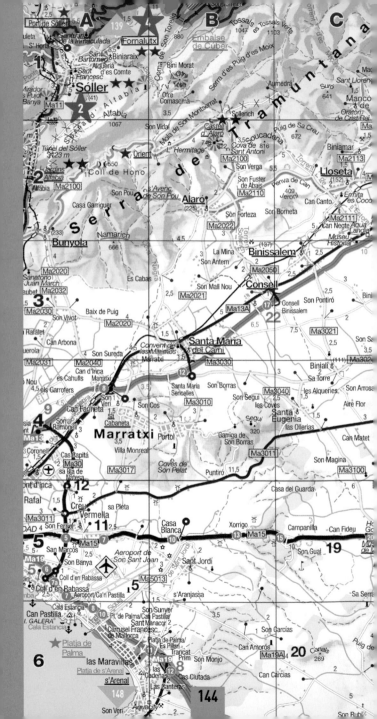

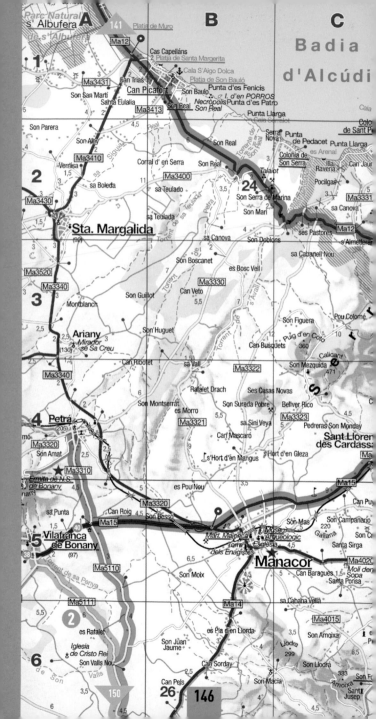

This map shows the following labeled locations:

Cap de Ferrutx

Punta Ferrutx
Talaia Moreia
432
Punta Trinquet d'es Moro
Punta dés Caló
es Caló
Cala Fosca
es Single
Caló de Penya Rotja
Farrayó de Aubarca
Puig Tudosa
3 436
Platja de Font Salada
58
Cala Matzocs
Cala Estreta
Cala Mitjana
Cala Torta
Punta del Buch
Cap des Freu
Cala Mesquida
Morei
561
Can Vicens
Betlem
Aubarca
Parc Natural de

ta d'es Barraca
Cala Mata
Betlem
mra de Betlem
St. Pere
4,5
Can Son Morey
Can Monseriu
Moleta de Ley
sa Vinysa
sa Cova
405
Son Mesquida Nou
Cala Mesquida
Jaumei
Punta de Na Foguera
Cala Moltó

nínsula de Llevant
Son Sancho
sa Duaya
es Recó
Collado d'es Castellats
Son Terrasa
Son Jaumell
Can Molto
Cala Guya
Cala Rajada
Torre Embucada
Punta de Capdepera

Son Sureda
Son Forteza
Son Fortunay
sa Campana
Santuari de Sant Salvador
7,5
Capdepera
Castell Capdepera
Ma15
Son Moll
2,5
Son Moll
Pedruscada
Punta des Farayos

Artà
1,5
Can Sureda
s'Hort
Mesquida
3,5
Talaiot de ses Paisses
180
Ma4042
Ma4041
Can Lloret Redó
257
5,5
Torrent de Canyamel
Son Febre
Son Forà
s'Heretat
Son Besso
Font de sa Cala
Cala Carregador
Punta del Carregador
Cala de sa Font
Punta del Fondal
Recó d'Estanté
Punta d'es Marás
Cova d'es Vells Marins

Sauma Vell
Can Cursal
sa Jordane
sa Coma Saquera
Ma4040
es Rafalet
es Rafel d'Albaix
Torre de Canyamel
Son Cavila
Can Caragol
Platja de Canyamel
2,5
Casa del Guardo
185
Racó d'en Massot
Coves d'Artà

Ma15
Cas Xiclati
Can Sopa
Ma4031
6,5
Jordi
315
Costa de Canyamel
Cap Vermell
Cala Canyamel
Cala Rotja

uero
182
Puig des Corp
370
es Costa des Pins
2,5
Platja d'es Ribell
Cap d'es Pinar

Son Servera
Port Vell
Caseria Port Nou
Port Verd
Son Corp
Cala Bona
Bahía de Artà

Can Pocofarina
Ma4030
7
Puig de Sa Font
271
182
Corp
2,5
Cala Bona

4022
es Rafal Sèch
182
Atalayas
sa Torre Nova
Cala Millor
Cala Millor
Arenal de Son Servera

Son Carrió
Safari Zoo
Cala Nao
1,5
Sa Coma
Punta de n'Amer
5
Platja de sa Coma
Cala Moreya
Sa Punteta
Cala Moreya
Can Bordils 1,5
s'Illot
Cala Mosca
MAR

Ma4024
Ma4023
Cala Morlanda
Punta de Sa Roca
Cala Morlanda
Punta Rasa
Cala Petita

2,5
els Hams
Ma4014
rtocristo Nou
Acuario
Portocristo
Cala Manacor
Cala Murta
Coves del Drac
Cala Mendana
Cala Anguila
MEDITERRÀNIA

5
Punta Reina
Cala Estany
Moro
Frontón d'es Mulá
Cala Falcó
Cala Varques
Punta d'es Llevants

4 km
2.5 mi

D E F

1
2
3
4
5
6

11

147

A   **B**   **C**

Sarria 4
143
Can Font
Son Figuerola
Can A bona
Son Sureda
Convent de
Miramos
Matxi
Establimer
Sarria
Estanglim
Nous
Son Bibiloni
Ma2031
Ma2040
Son Llado
Cas
Tixado Nou
es Cahults
Marafxi
Sant
Son Cos
Can Amoros
Cas Metje
Son Sardina
4 els Garroters
Can Farineta
Son Veri
Son Berga
Pureza
Ma1110
Son Masia
Es Pont
Son
Ramonell
Sa
Cabaneta
Bella Vista
Secar
del Real
la Real
la Victoria
Ma11
d'Inca
Ma13
Marratxi
Villa Monreal
Portol
Son Anglada
Indioteria
Coronell
Cas Capità
Ma30
sa Pla de
Natesa
Ma3017
Coves
Son Pel
Son Vida
Valldemossa
Soller
Son Estaca
Pont d'Inca
10
Ma20
Inca
Placa de
Toros
Rafal
Creu
Vermella
sa Pleta
Poblet
Espanyol
11
LA SOLEDAD
Ma3011
Son Ferriol
Ma15
Casa
Blanca
2
Castell de
Bellver
La Llotja
Catedral
San Marcos
Aeroport de
Son Sant Joan
10
Génova
6
Rosetta
Ma19
Son Banya
9
EL TERRENO
Cala
Cala
Portit
EL MOLINAR
Coll d'en Rabassa
Ma5013
Son Sunyer
5
12
Torre d
Pelaires
Ciudad Jardin
Platja Ciudad Jardin
Aeroport/Ca'n Pastilla
Cala Gamba
Son Manacor
Platja de Palma
Es Pillar
8
PALMA
(CIUTAT DE
MALLORCA)
Can Pastilla
I. GALERA
Cala Estancia
Pl. de Palma/Can Pastilla
Sant Manacor
Carrusel Francesc
de Mallorca
las Maravillas
11
12
★★   (33)
★ **Platja de**
Palma
las
Cadenas
las
Cantera
Platja de s'Arenal
s'Arenal
B a d i a   d e   P a l m a
Son Veri
Aquacity
4
Cala Blava
Cala Blava
Bella
Vista
Cap Enderrocat
Fuerte
ses Palmeres
Ma6014
es Puntarró
Son Granada
d'Abaix
Punta Negra
Cala Vella
ses Ollos
la Moreria
sa Torre
Badia A.
sa Torre
Racó de'n Casetes
Marsa
Badia Blava
Badia Grande
5   **M A R**
Tolleric
el Dorado
Cap de Regana
Caló de s'Arena
Can Miquel Batle
Fortin
M E D I T E R R À N I A
Ma6014
6   4 km
     2.5 mi
Punta Llobera
Maó (Menorca)
Cap E

148

This is a map of the Mallorca region showing the area around Algaida, Montuïri, Llucmajor, and the surrounding towns.

Towns and places:

Sencelles (118) 3 · Cas Canar · Santua... Conc...
Biniali · Sa Torre · Ma3020 · 145 · F
les Alqueries · Son Arrosa · Lear 4,5 · Ma3140 · Benas...
Ma3040 · Aire Flor · Ruberts · Lloret de Vista Alegre (201)
Son Segui · les Coves 2,5 · Can Xota 3,5 · Ma3011
Santa Eugenia · las Ollerias 1,5 · Can Matet 3 · Son Gat · Ma3140 · Ma3130 · Son Cervera 3,5
Ma3011 · Son Magina · Son Amora · Pina (153) · E S P l a
Ma3100 · Ma3110 · Son Moll · Son Llubi
Casa del Guarda 6 · Son Colá · Son Mezquida Nou 5,5 · Company 98 · Ma3230 · Son Tagam...
Campanilla · Can Fideu · Homes Gordiola · Ma3130 · Ma3131 · Son Mayol · Ma3200 · Ma3201 · Montuïri
Ma15 · Son Gual 10 · 19 · Museu de Vidre · Algaida (195) · Ma15 · 27 · 28 (188)
Esglèsia · Ermita de la Pau · Son Coll Vey · Ma5017 · Castellitx 3,5
Sa Serra · Aubenya · Son Ribas
Son Carcias · Can Arnau · Puig de Randa · Santuari de la Mare de Déu de Cura · sa Maimona
Can Amoros · Ma19A · Puig de Galdent 420 · Randa · Santuari de Sant Honorat · Puig de Ses Rocas 356 · 7,5
20 · Canals 269 · Ma5018 · Ma5010 · Santuari de N.S. de Gràcia · sa Bastida · Famelia
Can Carcias
Son Rubi · Llucmajor (143) · Ma5020 · de Serra de Montiss...
Son Cambeya · Talaiot · Mulet 263 · 4
13 · Son Noguera · s'Estanyol · Son Mulatet
Son Yeneboi · Son Gugulut Descals · 14 · Son Saletas · Ma19
Son Antem · Ma6015 · Son Segui · s'Alqueria Rotja
Son Guixá · Son Marranet · Revallat · 5
Son Mateu · Son Catany · sa Talaia · Can Barret · Can Roch
Talaiot · Garonda · sa Sorda
Capocorb · Ma6014 · Capocorb Vell · Vernisa · Vinyoleta · Moli · Can
sa Bassa Plana · Son Bielo · sa Barrala · Ma6030
ses Coves Prehistòriques · Cala Pi · Vallgornera · es Pas · s'Estanyol de Migjorn · Can Mandana · sa Ràpita · Can Estela · Cas Coix 4
Cala Pí · Ma6021 · 150 · sa Barrala Nova
Punta de Cala Beltràn · 149 · Racó de s'Arena · C'an...rbut · Platja de la Ràpita · ses Covetes

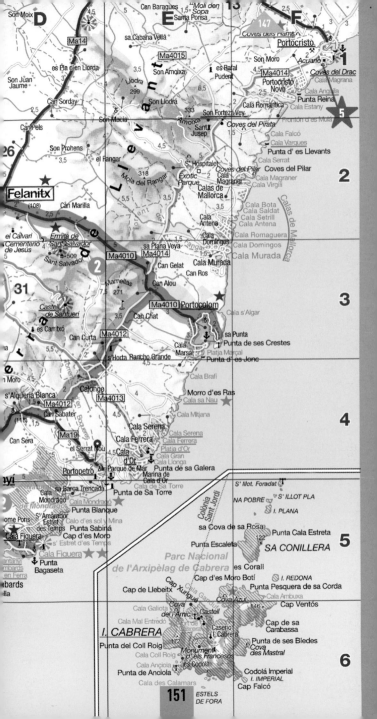

KEY TO ROAD ATLAS

Autobahn · Gebührenpflichtige Anschlussstelle · Gebührenstelle · Anschlussstelle mit Nummer · Rasthaus mit Übernachtung · Raststätte · Kleinraststätte · Tankstelle · Parkplatz mit und ohne WC	Trento 11	Motorway · Toll junction · Toll station · Junction with number · Motel · Restaurant · Snackbar · Filling-station · Parking place with and without WC
Autobahn in Bau und geplant mit Datum der Verkehrsübergabe	Datum Date	Motorway under construction and projected with completion date
Zweibahnige Straße (4-spurig)		Dual carriageway (4 lanes)
Fernverkehrsstraße Straßennummern	14 E45	Trunk road Road numbers
Wichtige Hauptstraße		Important main road
Hauptstraße · Tunnel · Brücke	)=(	Main road · Tunnel · Bridge
Nebenstraßen		Minor roads
Fahrweg · Fußweg		Track · Footpath
Wanderweg (Auswahl)	------	Tourist footpath (selection)
Eisenbahn mit Fernverkehr		Main line railway
Zahnradbahn, Standseilbahn		Rack-railway, funicular
Kabinenschwebebahn · Sessellift		Aerial cableway · Chair-lift
Autofähre · Personenfähre	•	Car ferry · Passenger ferry
Schifffahrtslinie		Shipping route
Naturschutzgebiet · Sperrgebiet		Nature reserve · Prohibited area
Nationalpark · Naturpark · Wald		National park · natural park · Forest
Straße für Kfz. gesperrt	X X X X X	Road closed to motor vehicles
Straße mit Gebühr		Toll road
Straße mit Wintersperre	XII-II	Road closed in winter
Straße für Wohnanhänger gesperrt bzw. nicht empfehlenswert		Road closed or not recommended for caravans
Touristenstraße · Pass	Weinstraße 1510	Tourist route · Pass
Schöner Ausblick · Rundblick · Landschaftlich bes. schöne Strecke		Scenic view · Panoramic view · Route with beautiful scenery
Heilbad · Schwimmbad		Spa · Swimming pool
Jugendherberge · Campingplatz	△ X △	Youth hostel · Camping site
Golfplatz · Sprungschanze		Golf-course · Ski jump
Kirche im Ort, freistehend · Kapelle		Church · Chapel
Kloster · Klosterruine		Monastery · Monastery ruin
Synagoge · Moschee	☆	Synagogue · Mosque
Schloss, Burg · Schloss-, Burgruine		Palace, castle · Ruin
Turm · Funk-, Fernsehturm		Tower · Radio-, TV-tower
Leuchtturm · Kraftwerk		Lighthouse · Power station
Wasserfall · Schleuse		Waterfall · Lock
Bauwerk · Marktplatz, Areal	• □	Important building · Market place, area
Ausgrabungs- u. Ruinenstätte · Bergwerk	⚒	Arch. excavation, ruins · Mine
Dolmen · Menhir · Nuraghen	π ◊ ⚭	Dolmen · Menhir · Nuraghe
Hünen-, Hügelgrab · Soldatenfriedhof	☆ ⊞	Cairn · Military cemetery
Hotel, Gasthaus, Berghütte · Höhle	⌂ ∩	Hotel, inn, refuge · Cave

Kultur
Malerisches Ortsbild · Ortshöhe	WIEN (171)	Picturesque town · Elevation
Eine Reise wert	★★ MILANO	Worth a journey
Lohnt einen Umweg	★ TEMPLIN	Worth a detour
Sehenswert	Andermatt	Worth seeing

Culture

Landschaft
German	Symbol	English
Eine Reise wert	★★ Las Cañadas	Worth a journey
Lohnt einen Umweg	★ Texel	Worth a detour
Sehenswert	Dikti	Worth seeing

Landscape

Ausflüge & Touren		**Trips & Tours**
Perfekte Route		**Perfect route**
MARCO POLO Highlight	★ 1	**MARCO POLO Highlight**

INDEX

This index lists all sights, museums and destinations plus the names of important people featured in this guide. Numbers in bold indicate a main entry.

WRITE TO US

e-mail: info@marcopologuides.co.uk

Did you have a great holiday?
Is there something on your mind?
Whatever it is, let us know!
Whether you want to praise, alert us
to errors or give us a personal tip –
MARCO POLO would be pleased to
hear from you.
We do everything we can to provide
the very latest information for your trip.

Nevertheless, despite all of our authors'
thorough research, errors can creep
in. MARCO POLO does not accept any
liability for this. Please contact us by
e-mail or post.

MARCO POLO Travel Publishing Ltd
Pinewood, Chineham Business Park
Crockford Lane, Chineham
Basingstoke, Hampshire RG24 8AL
United Kingdom

PICTURE CREDITS
Cover photograph: F1online: agefotostock (Bucht)
Images: DuMont Bildarchiv: Schwarzbach (114, 119, 120); F1online: agefotostock (1 top); © fotolia.com: diego
cervo (16 top); R. M. Gill (3 top, 3 bottom, 18/19, 23, 26 left 28/29, 56, 58, 60, 64/65, 66, 69, 71, 82/83,
106/107, 111, 125); R. Hackenberg (3 centre, 46, 74/75, 121); © iStockphoto.com: Joshua Hodge Pho-
tography (17 bottom), Motreal Photos (16 bottom); G. Jung (34, 100); Jörg Klausmann (17 top); Laif:
Celentano (50), Heuer (27), Zanettini (30 top); mauritius images: AGE (43, 88, 112/113), Alamy (2
top, 2 centre top, 4, 6, 7, 9, 63, 98/99, 102/103, 109, 116/117, 124 top, 124 bottom, 136/137), Beck
(5); mauritius images/imagebroker: Fuchs (26 right), STELLA (8); Mega Sport Centre (16 centre);
P. Rossbach (1 bottom, 97); O. Stadler (cover left, cover right, 2 centre bottom, 2 bottom, 15, 20, 32/33, 44, 53,
54/55, 68/69, 91, 94, 105, 110); T. Stankiewicz (13, 76, 92); The Travel Library/LOOK-foto (30 bottom); E. Wrba
(10/11, 24/25, 28, 29, 37, 39, 40/41, 48/49, 61, 73, 79, 81, 84, 85, 86/87, 95, 120/121, 131)

1st Edition 2012
Worldwide Distribution: Marco Polo Travel Publishing Ltd, Pinewood, Chineham Business Park,
Crockford Lane, Basingstoke, Hampshire RG24 8AL, United Kingdom. Email: sales@marcopolouk.com
© MAIRDUMONT GmbH & Co. KG, Ostfildern
Chief editor: Marion Zorn
Author: Petra Rossbach; Editor: Manfred Pötzscher
Programme supervision: Ann-Katrin Kutzner, Nikolai Michaelis, Silwen Randebrock
Picture editor: Gabriele Forst
What's hot: wunder media, Munich; Cartography road atlas: © MAIRDUMONT, Ostfildern
Cartography pull-out map: © MAIRDUMONT, Ostfildern
Design: milchhof : atelier, Berlin; Front cover, pull-out map cover, page 1: factor product munich
Translated from German by Kathleen Becker, Lisbon; editor of the English edition: John Sykes, Cologne
Prepress: BW-Medien GmbH, Leonberg
Phrase book in cooperation with Ernst Klett Sprachen GmbH, Stuttgart, Editorial by Pons Wörterbücher

DOS & DON'TS

There are a few things you should keep in mind during your visit to Mallorca

HIKING UNPREPARED

Don't underestimate the dangers of mountain hikes; they often start at sea level and go up beyond 1000 m. Don't head for the mountains without a hiking guide (human or in book form); leave word at the hotel where you're going, and make sure you have all the necessary gear (hiking footwear, raingear, sun protection, water, etc.) with you.

RIP-OFF CARRIAGE RIDES

Not every carriage driver has the same definition of ‚guided tour' as you. Agree the price before you start out and don't pay more than 40 euros for half an hour.

CARNATION LADIES

In tourist hotspots of Palma and other places you will encounter women aggressively offering carnations. In nearly all cases these are *gitanas* acting in groups. Firmly refuse and watch your bag or purse. These ‚ladies' are experts at their job!

DICING WITH DEATH

The dangers of swimming in the sea when the red flag is flying can't be stressed enough. Every year, lives are lost through carelessness or valiant efforts to save careless people. When there's a strong swell, undertows can become lethally dangerous. Be careful around finca or hotel pools too: over a dozen children drown each year be-

cause their parents don't pay attention!

PRICELESS FISH PLATTERS

Be careful when ordering fish or seafood if the restaurant doesn't display the price on the menu! This can lead to unwelcome surprises. Fresh seafood is a rare delicacy which even in Mallorca doesn't come cheap. Have your meal weighed in advance and ask for the kilo price!

BEING A KNOW-ALL

A laid-back attitude is a part of the Mallorcan mentality. There are limits though when foreigners act like big shots and treat their hosts like lackeys. Know-alls and show-offs don't cut it with the locals. And watch what you say: many understand English perfectly well!

THE CUP SCAMS

On the Platja de Palma in particular, but also in other places, you will come across con artists offering a game involving three cups and a pea. Plants in the audience suggest winning is possible. Stay away from these crooks – they'll scarper as soon as the police arrives. Many naive holidaymakers have lost money!